WITHOUT A HOMELAND

Love, Loss and
Resilience at
Qatrom Refugee Camp

BOBBIE LORD

Seascapes Press

Without a Homeland: Love, Loss and Resilience at Qatrom Refugee Camp
Copyright © 2022 by Bobbie Lord
All rights reserved. No part of this book may be used or reproduced in any manner whatsoever without written permission except in the case of brief quotations in the context of critical articles or reviews.

ISBN 979-8-9856024-0-1 (paperback)
ISBN 979-8-9856024-1-8 (ebook)

Cover photo by Bobbie Lord
Cover design by Aaxel Author Services & Deividas Jablonskis
Interior design by Aaxel Author Services

Printed in the United States of America

To my sons, Will and Geoff Moore - Will, who always challenged my thinking and pushed me out of my comfort zone to dare to plunge into the unknown, and Geoff, who always reminded me to laugh, to have fun and to enjoy the process. I am blessed with such wonderful sons.

Contents

Beginnings	1
Arrival	7
Group Living	11
Albanian Interpreters and Refugee Volunteers	15
Pit Latrines and Tent Showers	19
Money and Materials	21
British KFOR	23
Hounded by the Press	27
Interview Excerpts from Stuart News. Stuart, FL 11 May 1999	29
All in a Day's Work	35
Snippets of a Day	39
Hospitality amid Tragedy	45
Fatigue	47
Evening Break	51
Meeting at the Prefekture	53
Complaints	55
All Work and No Play	59
Three Unexpected Gifts	61
Children at Play	65
A Gentle Giant	69
United States Delegation	73
Medicos del Mundo, Spain	75
School Dilemma	77
Leisure Time	81
Inspection by Kosovar Refugees	83
War Crimes and an RI Officer	85
In the Words of Children	89
A Day Off	95
Facts, Facts, Facts	97

Secret Service Police, the Bread Saga, and Other Interruptions	101
Questions from a Friend	105
Asking for the Impossible	107
Some Days Are More Difficult than Others	109
Morava Mountains	111
Sensitive Topics	113
Children's Football Tournament	115
Bucket Brigade	117
Qatrom Art Exhibition	121
Explosion	123
Tragedy Strikes	125
Goodbye Party for British KFOR	129
Not on My Watch	131
Dignitaries Visit Qatrom	137
Rain, Rain, Rain	141
Let Me Entertain You	143
It's Over—Agreement Signed	147
Busloads of Refugees	149
An Interruption	151
Lake Ohrid	153
In Limbo	155
What to Expect—A Conversation with My Son, Will, 24 June 1999	157
Landmine Training	161
The Last Night	165
Waving Goodbye	169
A Promise Kept	171
Homeward Bound	175

Glossary of Terms

Argëtim: Fun in Albanian.

Buka: Bread in Albanian.

CARE: An NGO helping people affected by conflict and armed violence, famine and disasters.

Dorkas: Dutch NGO.

ICRC: The International Committee of the Red Cross, established in 1863, helping people affected by conflict and armed violence.

German Red Crescent: The German branch of the Red Cross.

Faleminderit: Thank you in Albanian.

Gabini më: My fault in Albanian.

KFOR: Kosovo Force, the NATO troops: British KFOR and French KFOR helped in Qatrom

Korçë, A town in Albania.

Kukës: A Town in northeastern Albania.

Lamtumirë: Goodbye in Albanian.

Medicos del Mundo: Medical NGO from Spain.

Më vjen keq: I am sorry in Albanian.

Më fal: Forgive me in Albanian.

Mirë: Good in Albanian.

Mirë dita: Good day in Albanian

Mirëmbrema: Good afternoon in Albanian.

Mirëmëngjes: Good morning in Albanian.

Natën e mirë: Good night in Albanian.

NATO: North Atlantic Treaty Organization, an intergovernmental military alliance between 30 North American and European Countries.

NGO: A non-governmental, not for profit organization to address humanitarian issues.

OSCE: The Organization for Security and Cooperation in Europe with 57 States in Europe, Central Asia and North America

Prefekt: The chairman of the local government council in Albania.

Prefekture: The name of the local government council in Albania.

Qatrom: Name of the Kosovar Albanian refugee camp in Korçë, Albania

RI: Relief International, a non-governmental organization that works with refugees, conflict, natural disasters and chronic poverty. RI employed me as manager of Qatrom.

Save the Children: An NGO humanitarian organization for the health and welfare of children.

Slobodan Milošević: President of Serbia (1989-1991); President of Yugoslavia (1997-2000).

The Hague: International Criminal Court, Hague, Netherlands.

Tung: Hello in Albanian, a shortened version.

UNHCR: United Nations High Commission for Refugees, the branch of the United Nations that deals with refugees.

Un jam Gjyshe: I am a grandmother in Albanian.

WFP: World Food Program, a United Nations program.

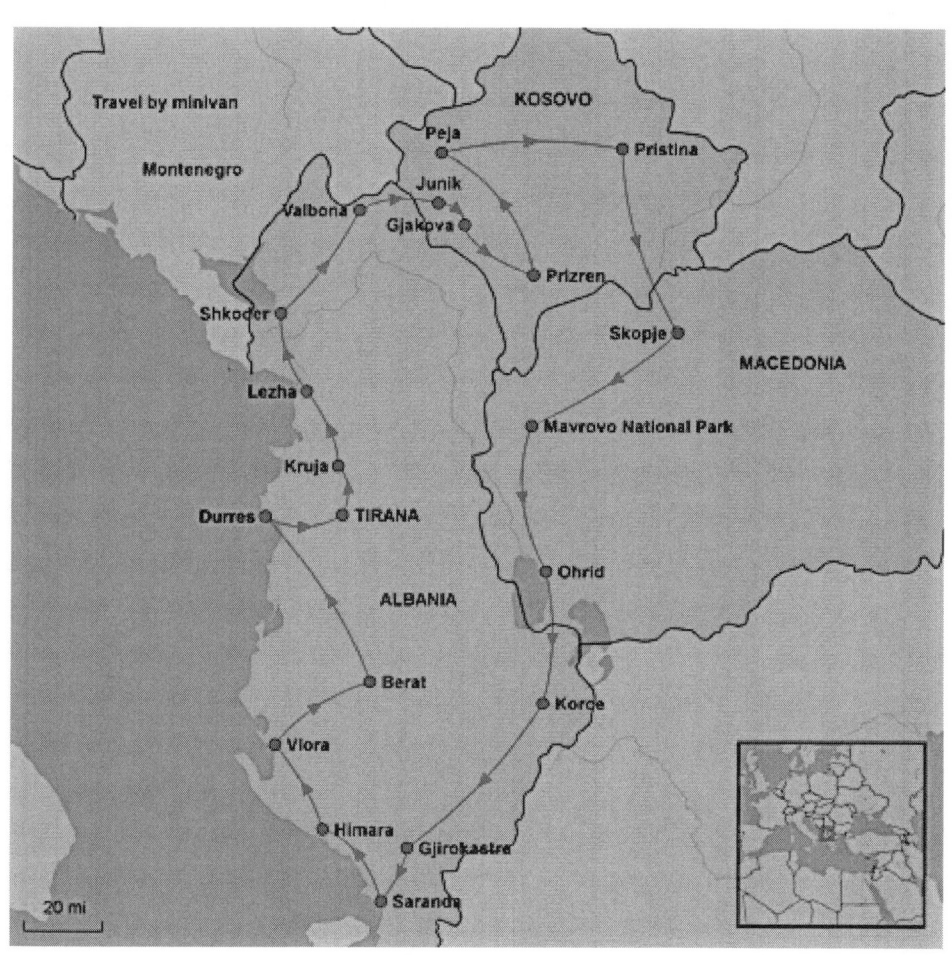

Map of the Balkan Region

"None who have always been free can understand the terrible fascinating power of hope of freedom to those who are not free."

— *Pearl S. Buck*

Beginnings

Plagued by boredom. A lost sense of purpose and uprooted after many moves. This was me in 1995 when I moved to Stuart, Florida to put down roots near my father after my mother's death. I then took an overseas assignment in Zambia with Habitat for Humanity. While I was away, my father died. I returned to Florida with no father, no community, no sense of belonging. And I needed a job. But what?

In late winter of 1999, as the news of the Kosovo crisis began to dominate the media, I paid attention. The Kosovo Liberation Army (KLA) had initiated attacks in February 1998 against the Serbian forces. Serbia controlled Kosovo and the KLA attacks brought the Yugoslavian military into Kosovo under Slobodan Milošević. The crisis raged, and refugees fled by the thousands from Kosovo to Macedonia and Albania when the NATO bombing started. Pressure mounted on the U.S. government to become involved, and with it, my longing to return to refugee work. I found purpose, adventure and fresh perspective — a place to grow, contribute, and focus on justice and human rights when working with refugees. It was May 1999, and I would turn sixty in the fall. Was I too old? I would never know unless I tried.

Would I be accepted if I found an organization working in Albania or Macedonia? I knew that Relief International (RI), a non-governmental organization (NGO) headquartered in Los Angeles, CA, responded to emergencies worldwide to assist refugees in crisis. Did they have openings? With the aid of the internet, I learned RI had five available positions to work in the field as a camp manager overseeing the refugees, Albanian staff and other NGOs working in the camps. (All NGOs working with refugees were under the umbrella of the United National High Commissioner for Refugees, (UNHCR)). Within an hour, I had applied. I had held management positions and done fieldwork in the IFO Refugee Camp, Dadaab, Kenya—among the largest refugee camps in the world in 1991. I crossed my fingers. Within three days of sending my application, a job offer arrived to join RI as part of the management team in Albania. I was elated. I had never worked in the Balkans or a post-Communist county. What would I find and learn?

With no time to research the area and one day to pack before my flight from Miami to Tirana, Albania, I had to focus on getting ready to go for an undetermined amount of time—maybe six months, maybe longer. Clothes, toiletries, and medicines for a six-month contract and three different seasons stuffed into one suitcase, my condo closed, and utility bills deducted with autopay, and I was off. This new adventure filled me with a sense of purpose and the opportunity to learn, experience, and serve others. As I was about to board my flight, a local TV reporter, sent by RI headquarters, stopped me and asked questions about the refugee situation in Albania. Unable to tell him much, I scurried to board the plane.

I settled in my seat for the long flight. In a blink of an eye, I was hurled back in time to June 1991, when I boarded a Pan American flight to Nairobi, Kenya, for my first refugee and humanitarian work experience. What started me on this path? How had I, at age fifty-two, dared to take a leap of faith into the unknown? The feelings of abandonment from ending a twenty-six-year marriage in 1987 and a job loss in California due to downsizing in 1990 overpowered me, I remembered. Fear left me reeling—numb, indecisive, and directionless. Now what? How was I going to support myself? The question tapped into my greatest fears and insecurities. A quick answer came when my son, Will, who was completing his doctoral program at the University of Colorado, Boulder, called. His six-month-old son, Kristopher, had developed a rare form of epilepsy, and they needed help with his care. A friend connected me with the owner of a company in Boulder where I could work part-time besides caring for Kris. I packed my car and drove to Boulder in the spring of 1990. I felt happy, useful, and content until Will accepted a teaching position at the University of California upon graduation with his doctoral degree in Political Science in 1991. I was thrilled for him, but my reason for being in Boulder disappeared. Depression, insecurity, and doubt settled over me like a heavy woolen cloak. Desperate, I had a brief chat with God—pleading with Him to give me something to do or let me die. Burdened with the prospect of starting over again, I cried, "Please not again." From nowhere, the desire to work in Kenya emerged as the answer. With Will's help, I applied for a position with Visions in Action for an internship in Nairobi, Kenya. I did not know where I would live or what the internship would look like, but I decided to take a leap of faith. Confident, I knew God led me to the right place. The flight attendant broke my reverie with the beverage cart. I smiled to myself as I ate my meal—forever grateful for the courage to leap into the unknown.

Exhausted after two days of travel, I arrived at the RI field headquarters in Tirana for a briefing and stayed overnight. Tirana, the capital of Albania, is known for its colorful Ottoman-era architecture surrounded by mountains and hills. At my briefing, Farshad, head of mission in Albania, told me that my assignment would be in Qatrom Refugee Camp, in Korçë. I would leave the following morning, 7 May 1999. Marcel, an Albanian staff driver from Tirana, drove me on a roughly 100-mile journey. I was delighted to leave the muddy roads and hot city of Tirana. We traveled southeast along narrow streets, some paved, some not, through the rugged mountainous landscape. We passed several small villages and beautiful countryside, dotted with concrete and steel bunkers, which stood like giant overgrown mushrooms.

"Marcel, what are those? Why are there so many?" I asked.

"They were constructed to protect Albania from any foreign invasion during the communist period—all 173,000 of them! They were never used and are now abandoned to deteriorate. They are ugly reminders of invasions during Albanian's long history." Sensing my curiosity, he asked, "Want to see one up close?"

"Yes." I approached the small, cobwebbed entrance, cautiously. It glittered with pieces of broken glass. I heard Marcel laughing when I refused to go inside—I noticed he had not volunteered to go inside one either.

We had a good laugh as we continued southwest and reached Lake Ohrid, which forms the border between eastern Albanian and the southwest part of Macedonia. With its magnificent shades of cobalt blue, the lake sparkled and shimmered as the sun danced on the surface. The eighteen-mile-long lake beckoned, but Marcel urged us to stay *en route*. He reminded me I could visit the lake on days when I had time off.

As we drew closer to the camp, I pondered about what I would find there—the Albanian people, the staff, the housing, and the condition of the refugees. Would they be as open and welcoming as the Albanian staff had been in Tirana?

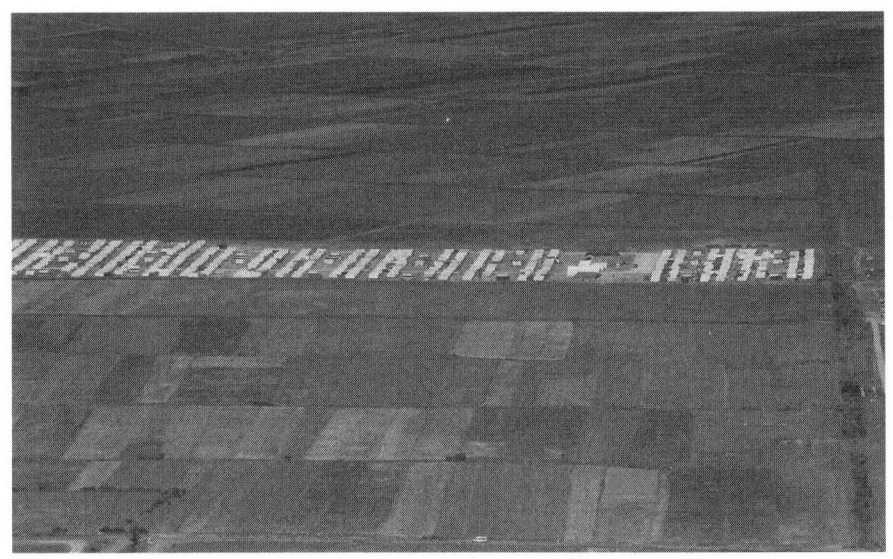

Aerial view of Qatrom Refugee Camp

RI Compound

Arrival

We stopped at the staff house assigned to the national and international teams before heading to Qatrom. For the next six months, my home was a two-story narrow, stucco building. The office and the medical staff were on the first floor, accessed by an external staircase. Our bedrooms, living room, kitchen, and bathroom were on the second floor. The building was sturdy and functional. It had the basics, running water and toilets. Similarly styled houses lined the paved, tree-lined road. The house overlooked a park and grassy playground for children and their mothers. It offered a cheerful and peaceful scene.

Having helped me carry my things into the house, Marcel said he would take me to Qatrom, approximately eight kilometers (five miles) away. Along the way, I noticed most of the apartments and houses had satellite dishes, which I learned were used to watch Italian television, which provided more variety than the Albanian stations. Next, we approached the center of Korçë, where four streets converged into a rotary. Vendor stalls selling clothes, kitchenware, and miscellaneous items and shops, selling saddles, bridles, and other equipment for horses and donkeys teemed with activity. There was also a blacksmith shop on a side street. Traffic slowed as old wooden carts hauled by donkeys caused a traffic jam. Shattering the tranquility of this nineteenth century scene, the loud horn of a Mercedes blared, and tires screeched as an impatient driver swerved around the carts. *What was a Mercedes doing in that pastoral setting? Must be one of the government officials or businesspeople.*

From the center, a narrow dirt road led to the refugee camp two kilometers away. High chain-linked fencing outlined the camp's perimeter. From my experience, I knew it provided safety and protection for the refugees—not to keep the refugees *in,* but to keep unauthorized people *out.* (The local residents often thought the refugees had more than they did.) As we arrived, a guard grunted as he pushed the heavy gate open. Dust billowed in the air as the gate scraped the dirt. Inside, a very long gravel road, wide enough to accommodate trucks, extended from one end of the camp to the other, approximately one to two acres total of flat, dry farmland. Typically, UNHCR negotiated for land use with the host country or local government. Since the local authorities would not negotiate, UNHCR had negotiated with a local farmer.

First, I asked Marcel to stop at the management compound, separated in a self-enclosed area, where four huge tents (ten meters by thirty meters) housed Relief International, The German Red Crescent (Red Cross), the Salvation Army, and a storage tent. I introduced myself to the staff inside the RI tent. I met Marci from the U.S. and four Albanian interpreters: Xhilda, Genti, Elton, and Indrit. After a bit of small talk, Marci offered to help me jump right into work by giving me a tour of the camp.

Marci had a wide grin, perfect teeth and dimpled cheeks. Her long blond hair, tied in a ponytail, swayed from side to side as she walked. As we exited the compound, she turned to me and said, "I arrived the third week in April and have been on the run ever since. The camp was still being built when the first refugees arrived. I have lost fifteen pounds running from one end of the camp to the other. I'm glad you are here."

We continued to chat as we walked along. Row after row of new sparkling white tents stood like soldiers standing in formation, as far as the eye could see. Between tent sections were pit latrines, water taps and tent showers. I also noticed a tall, thick tree with an expansive canopy, wearing fresh green leaves of spring. A gentle breeze caused them to flutter. That lone tree became a central gathering point and would provide welcome shade as the leaves matured.

The organization and the order of the camp impressed me. Incredibly, given the humanitarian crisis before me, my senses filled with pleasure as the sun shone on me, and white fluffy clouds filled the azure sky. The rugged, steep Morava Mountains around the camp added a sense of strength and stability. I snapped myself out of my thoughts—the scene appeared tranquil; yet I knew from experience fear, disorientation, doubt, and uncertainty lay beneath the surface. The refugees had just fled their homes, leaving the dead behind and separated from family members.

I noticed several refugees along the way. I could see their pain and suffering, loss, and grief on their faces and in their body postures. They carried the weight of dreadful memories—hunger, fear, and anger. They carried the acrid memory of the stench of burning houses, flesh, and gunpowder. They carried the ominous sound of marching boots, tanks rumbling on the pavement, bullets pinging off buildings, and screams of terror and pain. They carried fatigue and survivor's guilt. They carried the sounds, the smells, terror, and horrors of war. Within the following weeks, I learned of their desire for revenge to get even with the Serbs for forcing them to flee, for killing their loved ones and pillaging their homes. Revenge was a part of their culture. Yet, they yearned and hoped to return to their beloved Kosovo and a better, more peaceful life.

As I walked along between the rows of new tents and traumatized people, I heard the general hum of voices. The refugees seemed subdued; children clung to their parents. I encountered a few men. My heart was saddened. I knew my job would be to provide as much comfort and stability as possible. I tried to put myself in their shoes—torn from their homeland to live in a tent with only the basics of food, shelter, and medicine. These refugees did not want to live in crowded tents with pit latrines, communal showers, no electricity. There was no privacy except within the confines of their one-room tents with all the other family members. Several older people lived in the camp. How would they ever use a pit latrine?

Returning to the RI tent, I thanked Marci for the tour. Everyone had done an outstanding job organizing and getting the camp to function. Feeling the effects of jetlag, I told Marci I would head back to the house to rest. She invited me to join her for supper at a local restaurant where other international personnel gathered. On the drive back, the pain and suffering I had observed made me feel helpless, with every cell vibrating with the outrage of senseless war, oppression, and dominance. The words of Mahatma Gandhi "Be the change that you wish to see in the world," swirled in my head. My sense of purpose and service returned, as I remembered the words of Leo Buscaglia, "Too often we underestimate the power of a touch, a smile, a kind word, a listening ear, an honest compliment, or the smallest act of caring, all of which have the potential to turn a life around." I knew this would be my mantra for each day.

Group Living

I ran into challenges everywhere—language, refugees, group living, foreign country, no friends. Group living presented a particular set of difficulties, although we had nothing to complain about compared to the refugees. Our living accommodations were luxurious compared to tent living. Having never met, fourteen international and Albanian staff crammed into the offsite house with three to four people per bedroom. Four Albanian medical staff who served the local population, lived on the bottom floor next to the management office. The two available bathrooms, one on each floor, revolved like a swinging door with so many people. A water shortage in Korçë added another challenge—water was only available twice a day for four hours without enough hot water for showers (my solar shower became a lifesaver for me). At least we had hot water, while the refugees did not. Albeit the occasional pit bath never removed the dirt and fatigue. Although crowded, we enjoyed a unique camaraderie. RI soon realized additional housing was needed and rented a house for the Albanian staff.

Cold boxed cereal and instant Turkish coffee were the breakfast items and always eaten on the fly. I usually did not eat cereal, and

I was not a fan of instant Turkish coffee. However, we had access to a refrigerator to add items when time permitted. Each night, I would put my half-filled water bottle in the freezer to have cold water the next day. The staff and others teased me about the contents, as a cover kept the water cooler longer. The second week after my arrival, RI hired two cooks/cleaners for the house. Much to our delight, after working twelve to fourteen-hour days, a clean house and the aromas of well-cooked meals greeted us when we returned home. Hot dishes of lamb or goat with buttery steamed vegetables became the staple meal. On many evenings, delicious soups garnished with lemons filled us. Small salads and a dessert rounded each satisfying meal. Cold cereal seemed a small trade-off for such appealing dinners.

Another disadvantage of living in close quarters was that everyone wanted to use the internet to email family and friends. Frequent power outages added to the stress. Even with my personal laptop, I had to wait to use the one internet line to write and receive correspondence from home. Since I woke earlier than most, I would dash downstairs to plug into the internet. By the time everyone woke, I had finished. With only one telephone in the office and no telephone service at Qatrom, we relied on radios for communication—all before the cell phone era. The radio reception between the camp and the office was difficult and unreliable. Instead, drivers often had to take messages back and forth like modern day carrier pigeons. My only means of communication with my family and friends was email or handwritten letters, which took four to six weeks each way. As with any new situation, adjustments were required. Not speaking the Albanian language presented daily challenges, but in the group house, we all spoke English. The two-story house soon became home and we all adjusted to the minor inconveniences—grateful we had a house to live in, hot running water, nourishing prepared meals, and a place to unwind and relax after a stressful day.

RI Staff and Volunteers

Albanian Interpreters and Refugee Volunteers

What would it be like to work all day with interpreters? Would I ever learn enough words to communicate in the Albanian language? So many unknowns stood before me; yet I was excited to learn and work with my interpreters. Would one stand out more than another? I knew I had to depend on them and wanted to get to know each of them and develop a warm, working relationship.

Curious, I approached the interpreters gathered around someone. Elton was in the center holding forth. I observed his demeanor, which radiated leadership. I smiled as I saw the ease with which he laughed and joked. Elton lived in Tirana. His slight stature reminded me of a footballer (soccer player). He had dark, curly hair cropped close. His eyes were the color of dark roasted chestnuts. He had thick eyebrows, a prominent nose, and straight white teeth.

I asked, "Elton, what did you do before for RI?"

"I was in school," he said. "But I wanted to become a footballer. I was terrific as a forward, but my father wanted me to have an education and discouraged me from following my dream. I applied for a job with Relief International as an interpreter, and they sent me here. I'm delighted I came here and not Kukes or another refugee camp. I like the people I'm working with. Even though we just met, it feels like we have known each other for a long time."

"Yes, it looks like a wonderful, team, and I look forward to getting to know everyone better."

Xhilda lived with her family in Korçë. She was petite in stature, and mighty in spirit. A college student, she charmed everyone with her dimpled cheeks, cornflower blue eyes, and gentle demeanor. Her blond hair framed her pretty face like a halo. A genuine warmth emanated from her. Also, she had a remarkable command of the English language. I knew I could depend on her in so many situations, especially when dealing with women and girls and their particular needs. I knew she would translate with compassion and understanding with her openness, which allowed the women to discuss their needs with honesty and sincerity. RI wanted to eliminate one interpreter and I had to fight to keep Xhilda. Management didn't understand the necessity of having a female interpreter to work on women's issues. In the end, I won, and Xhilda stayed.

Before joining RI as an interpreter, soft-spoken, gentle Genti studied at the University of Tirana at the School of Journalism. He had short, strawberry blond curly hair. A reddish five o'clock stubble framed his cheeks and chin, and a mischievous grin appeared when his eyes crinkled with delight. His boyish charm made others feel comfortable—he was an asset to the team.

Lastly, there was Indrit, a good-looking college student from Tirana. He had a handsome face with a five o'clock shadow, broad shoulders, and a football player's athletic build. His stance gave the impression of confidence. He wore a baseball cap backwards. When he tilted his head, his eyes peered down his nose and he stood apart from the others. There was an arrogant air about him, giving off the impression that he didn't belong with the group. He held a cigarette in his right hand and he had little to offer during our discussion. *Okay, I thought this one would be a challenge. I wonder how willing he is to work.*

As we were making our introductions, a young refugee,

Kosovar, sauntered into the RI tent and asked in perfect English if he could volunteer to help us. He arrived with a red baseball cap on his head with the brim in the back. His eyes sparkled, and his wide grin showed perfect teeth. I asked him where he learned to speak such good English. He replied, "I watched American westerns on TV." He had the John Wayne swagger as he walked around the compound. His engaging smile, wit, and kind heart showed he was a born leader. We discussed the duties and how the volunteers would assist us in our daily operations. He said he would bring others after lunch to help with the distribution of jerry cans, which was planned for later in the afternoon.

As the days progressed, fifteen teenage refugee volunteers assisted us each morning to help with everything. Being typical teenagers, they strolled into the compound between 9:00 and 9:30 AM, still wiping the sleep from their eyes. Their willingness to help in every way enhanced each aspect of camp life. They were delightful young people. The office tent in the compound gave them a place to congregate. Although from different areas of Kosovo, deep friendships developed. Tribal differences disappeared. With tears in my eyes, I marveled as I observed the bonds between them strengthen and grow. They worked as a team and assisting us gave them focus and purpose. Of course, they still laughed and kidded around, as teenagers do, which lightened the atmosphere for all of us. Their youthful energy kept us going, especially on demanding days.

Learning to work with this delightful group of young people excited me. Although, some cultural differences challenged me. The Albanians nodded their heads up and down to signify "no" and from side to side to specify "yes". Would my brain adapt? Maybe they would help me? I had a wonderful feeling about this group. Their attitude of openness and willingness was such an asset to the RI team. I felt confident we would put the fun in each day amid the suffering and trauma around us. I knew I had found my purpose to grow and serve.

Bobbie and 2 refugees with pit latrines and shower tent in the background

Pit Latrines and Tent Showers

Walking along the camp's center road, I noticed unpainted wooden structures called pit latrines and tent showers wedged between the pristine, white tent sections of Qatrom. Each latrine had two doors and a rudimentary stencil drawing of a man or a woman. Inside, the walls were rough to the touch. It was dark, and the air was stifling and hot. Footholds over the hole accommodated the stance of a man, but not that of women and children.

During their group sessions with the medical staff, the women talked about feeling vulnerable while crouching over the gaping hole with its eight-foot drop. I related to their feelings of vulnerability. One bent nail locked the door closed for privacy. Also, being older with knee pain, I found it difficult to squat and felt unsteady with my feet planted wide on the footholds. I had to remember to bring toilet paper, as there was no place to put the toilet roll. My legs trembled as I rose from the squatting position with no hand railing, which needed to be installed—the German Red Crescent in charge of water and sanitation had yet to build them. I pushed them to create the bars after receiving complaints from the older and sick refugees. No one wanted to touch the floor to help get up. I nearly toppled over once when my radio, which was on my waistband, squawked. Small children required help to prevent them from tumbling down the hole. In the communal latrine outside our compound, I noticed bottles of water propped near the pit opening. I learned the Muslim community did not use toilet paper but used water to clean themselves.

The gap between the walls and the roof provided ventilation and light. With the uncovered hole, the stench of excrement permeated the air. The pits would be doused with hydrated lime, and disinfectant applied to the floor facilitated keeping the latrines as germ-free as possible. I never asked others to do what I was not willing to do. Needing volunteers to keep the latrines sanitized, I showed them how by donning a protective suit with a mask over my nose and mouth. I went from latrine to latrine and cleaned with the disinfectant. The spray from the disinfectant hose forced bloody stools and dysentery into the hole.

Tent showers hovered over flimsy wooden platforms as if daring the refugees to enter at their own risk. The refugees splashed themselves with cold water from a bucket and they bitterly complained about not having hot water. They felt vulnerable there too, with no security other than cloth ties to close the tent flaps. While walking to the latrine or showers at night, the potential threat of rape increased. The utility poles of the nearby town offered insufficient lighting.

Management discussed the vulnerability and possibility of rape with the medical staff at Medicos del Mondo. The medical staff recorded complaints and discussed safety procedures with the women, including the necessity of walking in pairs and carrying flashlights at night to help reduce the risks.

Money and Materials

Money, money, money—where did the refugees get money? Without the ability to work, the refugees had no means of obtaining cash unless they brought money with them, had a nearby relative, or sold some of their goods in the local market. The temptation to steal threatened the materials stored in unsecured tents. Theft happened. Strolling along the main road in Korçë, I noticed many UNHCR items for sale in the local stalls. Unable to determine how the materials disappeared, we assumed the refugees took them at night and sold them to local sellers for cash. Thefts occurred not only in Qatrom but in all the UNHCR warehouses, with medicine and drugs a priority. To combat the theft problem, we requested three lockable box-car containers. Theft would continue until we secured the material. For the ex-pats, procuring money presented challenges too. There was only one bank in Korçë and no available ATMs. I befriended a local teller who allowed me to cash traveler's checks. Most of my salary went into my home checking account, the balance I received in local currency from RI.

Unannounced deliveries were common. In one instance, three large moving vans arrived to deliver sleeping bags, plastic sheeting, cooking kits, and jerry cans for water storage. We were grateful for the material, although it was a logistical nightmare. We accepted all the needed items. If only we had time to prepare! Switching gears and constant disruptions were typical day in this refugee camp.

Change was perhaps the only constant. My adrenaline surged with the continuous upheavals, challenges, and the threat of danger. It was strangely addicting, although too much drained my energy. I felt alive and valuable—again, grateful for the opportunity to serve. Where else could I experience such immediate feedback? Immediate recognition that I made a difference to someone or a situation with a listening ear, a kind gesture, and an open heart and mind brought instant comfort and satisfaction.

British KFOR

*T*he sun peeked over the horizon. Early mornings brought tranquility before the chaos of the day. Dew speckled poppies painted the fields red. The smell of the rich, damp, freshly tilled soil filled the air. Spring was coming into full bloom. The days were growing warmer, although a morning chill lingered. Out of the corner of my eye as we drove, I saw a shepherd with a long, crooked staff in hand meander through the fields as he tended his sheep — like a scene from biblical times. I loved these moments of quiet while most of the refugees slept. Then the mechanical whop, whop, whop sound of rotating blades shattered the silence. We looked up, following the sound, and saw a helicopter appear over the mountain, heading straight towards us. What was a helicopter doing here? Puzzled, we ran to the fence to get a better look.

The grass flattened, and the dust spewed as the helicopter hovered over the adjacent field. Upon landing, a man in uniform emerged and walked directly towards us. He introduced himself as Brigadier General Alan of the British KFOR (Kosovo Force), which was a part of NATO. "We are going to set up our command station adjacent to Qatrom," he said. "Our mission here is to coordinate and protect the building of the other camps in the area before we go to Kosovo. Everything should be in place within a couple of days." With a brief nod, he turned and walked back to the helicopter to supervise the operation.

The stir awakened the refugees who were excited for a relief of boredom in the camp. They rushed to the fences to observe the swirling activity and the deafening sounds of the helicopters flying in and out. All day cranes and trucks arrived, filling the air with the clamor of construction. Machines pounded poles for the chain linked fencing. By late afternoon, fences topped with barbed wire enclosed their compound. An enormous satellite dish stood high on a metal tower. With each helicopter landing or takeoff, clouds of dirt and dust scattered everywhere. Large ten-meter by thirty-meter army tents popped up like balloons. As dusk approached, the frenzy lulled; the cranes and trucks pulled away. The entire compound teamed with activity—everything in place and secure. How did they assemble everything in one day?

The brigadier general returned to brief us on their progress. "I apologize if we created any disruptions. We will have a guard stationed here 24/7. At 0800, our troops will arrive."

"Yes, the activity created great excitement. It was an excellent diversion for the refugees, as they have little to do. And the extra protection and safety will give us peace of mind. We are all delighted that KFOR chose our site for the command post," I said.

The following day, 120 British KFOR personnel arrived. The hum of activity flourished, much to the delight of the refugees. At 1600 hours, a lieutenant strolled into the RI compound to invite us to attend their briefing, including a progress report on their activities and a weather update. After the meeting, we mingled with the troops for a few minutes.

The daily afternoon briefings provided a welcomed deviation from our typical day. No matter how exhausted or stressed we were, the presentations provided a respite and the chance to enjoy the company of other English-speaking ex-pats. Only then did we realize how fatiguing it was to think and speak all day through interpreters. We could feel the stress wash away as we sat and listened—luxuriating in the feelings of comfort.

We thanked the general for allowing us to attend the sessions, telling him the briefings provided a sanctuary, sense of normalcy, and relief from camp for a few minutes to relax and enjoy the company of his troops. He had done us an excellent service and provided extra security. He told me I came every day with a bright smile on my face like a ray of sunshine. He never guessed I was stressed. That remark made my day, and I guaranteed we would attend the daily briefings.

Hounded by the Press

Not the press again. How can we do our job if the press keeps hounding us? Today brought another interruption of our morning meeting. Fox News arrived and wanted to interview me with the tents as a backdrop. They asked question upon question regarding the number of refugees in the camp. When would the next busload of refugees arrive? How were they being treated? Explain camp life, etc. I didn't know the answers to many of the questions since I had only arrived at Qatrom three days earlier. I ended the interview after a half hour. The Fox reporter told me the piece would air in the U.S. that evening. I never learned if it did.

More press—BBC, Reuters, ABC, Voice of America, and NBC reporters annoyed us daily, clamoring for information about the expected arrivals of 6,000 refugees who were in Macedonia. At that time, Macedonia had closed their borders to Kosovar refugees. Day after day, the media hounded us. No sooner did one reporter with cameras leave when another arrived demanding information that we did not have. The interruptions became unbearable. The constant flow of reporters created enormous distractions from our duties.

Not liking to be the center of attention. I hated having the microphone thrust in my face as a reporter peppered me with questions. I felt uncomfortable and frustrated because we had no answers. During one interview, my radio squawked. The reporter tapped her foot on the dirt, folding her arms across her chest as I responded to the call.

With a shrug, I said, "I apologize. I need to attend to a situation. Please give me your contact information." The interview ended, much to the chagrin of the reporter. As I turned away, I tried to stifle a grin and added a skip to my step.

Since I understood the value of news media to draw attention to the plight of the refugees, I promised to contact each reporter when we received word about the expected arrival of the refugees from Macedonia. However, most of the busloads from Macedonia appeared without announcement. We scrambled to register them, distribute supplies and equipment, and assign them to tents—unified coordination amid chaos. We dropped everything to address the issue at hand, which became our daily motto.

Interview Excerpts from Stuart News. Stuart, FL 11 May 1999

Samuels: My name is Michael Samuels. I am a reporter from the Stuart News, working on a story about your work in Albania and your previous experience traveling for humanitarian efforts. Please answer the following questions: Why do you go to the various places to help, compared to sending donations of money or food?

Me: I love fieldwork and working directly with people from different cultures and ethnic backgrounds. I have been fortunate in my life, and I want to contribute by giving back to those less fortunate. I prefer donating my time directly. I also donate money to various organizations, non-governmental organizations that strive to lessen oppression, promote human rights and economic improvement.

Samuels: How has your experience been so far in Albania?

Me: My experience has been incredible so far. I arrived on 5 May. Relief International (RI), a humanitarian non-profit organization, hired me to be part of the management team at

Qatrom Refugee Camp in Korçë, Albania. Currently, we are expecting 6,000 Kosovar Albanians from Macedonia. RI is the overall camp management. We oversee three other NGOs who work in the camp. The German military built Qatrom, and Japan donated the tents. German Red Crescent, similar to our Red Cross, oversees the water and sanitation, while Oxfam, another NGO, supplied the hardware. Also, the Salvation Army prepares and stores the food, which was donated by the World Food Program (WHO). Medicos Del Mondo Spain provides medical services to the refugees. The cooperation between the NGOs has been outstanding. We have several Albanians helping in the camp with translation and logistics.

Samuels: What does your work consist of and how was it different from what you have done in the past in Kenya, Zambia, and Guatemala?

Me: As part of the management team, we oversee all other NGOs working here to ensure all the refugees' health and safety. We register all new refugees. Once registered, we assign equipment and tents to each family. We address all issues that arise, attend daily UNHCR briefings and work closely with the local government.

I love working with refugees, and I am grateful for this opportunity to be a part of the RI team. My work at UNHCR, Kenya, was similar when I worked in IFO Refugee Camp, Dadaab, Kenya, although my primary focus was managing a micro-credit program for refugees in Nairobi. I was the first in-country resource development officer in Zambia for Habitat for Humanity, to focus on in-county funding to build houses. I worked with businesses and embassies for funding and grants to get materials for houses and incoming generating projects. I received funds to build six boreholes, wells, to provide clean water with the help of the Zambian Rotary Club and embassies. We helped over 30,000 village people who had no access to clean water. I also guided community leaders in writing a proposal for a clinic in rural areas.

In Guatemala, I joined a group of thirteen women from all

over the U.S. to work with the Mayan women, who had just come out of thirty-six years of war. We taught meditation and trauma relief techniques within the two-week mission. We touched many lives while there.

Samuels: How successful do you feel you have been?

Me: I have made lasting friendships, which are very meaningful to me. I long to return to each place to learn about the development and to see old friends again.

Samuels: What have you experienced in Albania that has hindered the success of your mission?

Me: Supplies, such as cooking stoves, have not arrived. We still have no soap or shampoo. Theft of materials has been a problem. We have requested unused railroad cars, which can be locked to secure all equipment and materials. Complaints of food and *buka* bread, and not having meat and fresh vegetables are problems. Hot water is not available. There is no electricity in the camp. More counseling to deal with the trauma is needed. Since we rely on the donor community, funding is an issue. Points of entry and border crossings for all supplies are not always timely. Our primary concern is for the comfort, health, and safety of the refugees.

Samuel: What has helped make your job more successful?

Me: Without the extraordinary cooperation of everyone, including the other developmental NGOs that work in the area, we would be less effective.

Samuels: Describe the atmosphere of the camp. What it is like to deal with refugees who have been displaced from their families and homes.

Me: Qatrom has only been in existence for three weeks and the finishing touches are still being done, such as the water system, fencing, safety bars in the pit latrines. We have enormous tents for a school and a community center. Each cluster has elected community leaders—thirty-three clusters with twenty-four tents per cluster, one man and one woman elected per cluster. Self-management is key to the success of a camp. RI feels it is imperative to get the refugees involved immediately to give them a sense of control and empowerment. I work with the small board elected by the larger group.

We are at one-half of our capacity right now. Most refugees in Qatrom have come from Pristina and are well educated and used to spacious homes and furnishings. It is difficult to adjust to living in a tent, use communal bathing areas and pit latrines. The food, which is the standard of UNHCR, is not their usual diet, and the most traumatic has been the separation and killing of family members and their homes. I am finding the refugees warm, generous, and delightful despite what they have endured. I have a group of teenage refugees working with us. We are getting quite close and working as a family unit. Some are even calling me "mother."

Samuels: What kind of toll has it taken on you emotionally? Physically?

Me: Since I have worked with refugees before, I knew what to expect. Somehow, while in the situation, you look past the trauma and concentrate on the job at hand, supporting the refugees in whatever way is necessary. Very long days without a break are exhausting.

Samuels: How is this job easier or more challenging than the ones you have done in the past?

Me: I don't know yet.

Samuels: What is your opinion about NATO's mission and the constant bombing? Do you feel they should stop?

Me: I don't get involved with politics. I concentrate on the safety and security of the refugees in Qatrom.

Samuels: When do you think a peace agreement to stop the bombing and get the Yugoslavian troops out of Kosovo will happen?

Me: I have no idea. Our only information is through our daily UNHCR briefings. We do not have access to television or newspapers.

Samuels: Please add any additional comments you think I might have neglected to discuss you feel are pertinent and relevant to the story. Thank you very much for your time.

Me: I have nothing more to add. Thank you for your interest in Qatrom and the plight of the Kosovar refugees who had to flee from their beloved homeland.

Refugee woman doing her laundry

All in a Day's Work

How to involve the refugees and give them a sense of control? UNHCR emphasized that self-management was a crucial element for empowering the refugees with a sense of self-sufficiency, autonomy, and agency. Each cluster of twenty tents had to elect one man and one woman to represent them. Those representatives elected an overall board. Resistance and suspicion, instilled by the refugees' experience of communism under Tito and Serbia's authoritarian government, lingered with the Kosovar people. Knowing these obstacles as I worked with the board, I had to have patience, persistence, and understanding. Little by little, the barriers broke down.

When the board asked if we could meet daily, I sensed I had gained their trust. Together, we learned to build decision trees, using options and consequences. They wanted me to make all the decisions. I refused. I stressed that decisions could be altered, changed, or revised — nothing was set in concrete, but they had to be the ones to decide.

At lunch before such meeting, Xhilda approached me with lowered head and downcast eyes. "May I ask a question?"

"Of course."

"What do colors mean in a sentence, like blue?"

I smiled and placed my hand over my heart. "Blue can show when a person is sad, or if a person is shivering with cold. The context determines the meaning. Red might be anger, as in red with rage or embarrassment, or as her cheeks flushed red. Green could mean envy or illness—he looked green with envy, or he looked green around the gills."

Her eyes lit up. She nodded as the "aha" moment of clarity crossed her face—such a tender moment and lasting bond between us seared in my heart and memory. I was thrilled and touched at the opportunity to increase her understanding of the nuances of the English language. Moments like this gave me respite from the stresses of the day.

I was dreading my 1 PM meeting with the board, as I had a challenging discussion ahead about the picnic tables stolen the night before. Resistance rose like an ugly thorn in the discussion. Without a firm response, chaos would prevail. I stood leaning forward on the table and said, "There will be no more distributions until the tables reappear. However, there will be no retribution for those who took them."

By late afternoon, all the picnic tables resurfaced.

Still, chaos lurked around every corner. The distribution of beds was scheduled at 2:30 PM. I insisted at least one community leader attend. Anxiety, claustrophobia, and terror surged through me when a crush of refugees descended upon me. My mind flashed back to a football game in Kenya when President Daniel arap Moi opened the gates to all non-ticket holders. The force of a crowd hurled me against a fence with the barbed wire inches from my face—dozens of people were trampled to death in the stadium that day, but luckily, I survived uninjured.

"Move back!" I screamed. The crowd swelled closer and closer. Panicked, I grabbed a community leader who led me through the crowd. The distribution came to a screeching halt. Shaken, I marched to the management tent and demanded a board meeting to discuss distribution protocol. We needed a viable solution without stampedes and disorganization. We all agreed that all future distributions would be done by sections with committee members present.

After a late dinner and bone-weary, sleep tugged at me as I prepared for bed. Half undressed, the squawk of the radio jolted me. Busloads of refugees would arrive at 10 PM. No sleep yet. Pulling my clothes back on, I called the team to assemble. Yawning, we grabbed flashlights and lanterns, piled into the vehicle, and sped back to Qatrom. No sooner had we set up when three busloads of refugees arrived. By the time we finished registration, distributed equipment, and settled the refugees into their assigned tents, it was 2 AM. With an 8 AM meeting, sleep would be in short supply that night. Although exhausted and tense with fatigue, I recalled how small kindnesses—hugs and being called "mother of the camp" by the refugees. These, as always, rejuvenated me to face my early wake-up call.

Refugees arriving at Qatrom camp

Refugees registering at Qatrom camp

Snippets of a Day

Dawn approached as I lay awake. So many issues arose each day, not only in the camp but also during our UNHCR daily briefings. But despite all the thoughts swirling around in my head, I knew I belonged. I knew our work had an impact. To get a sense of what happened in one day, I decided to list my experiences, thoughts, and situations that needed to be addressed.

A mountain of rejected donated second-hand clothes:
- Clothes dumped everywhere
- Trash cans overflowed
- Pro-offered shoe refused — not Nikes
- Distribution ceased
- Bad attitudes
- Complaints continued

International Committee for the Red Cross (ICRC):
- Sent a team to Qatrom
- Brought radios for communication
- Refugees contacted family members remaining in Kosovo and Macedonia

- Refugees confirmed location at Qatrom and their safety
- Reunited scattered family members
- Family tracing critical

Relief International registration forms to help with reunification and the return, require fields.
- Names of family members in Qatrom
- Ages of family members in Qatrom
- Birthplace/home village of family members in Qatrom
- Last known place before Qatrom

Survey of Qatrom:
- Conducted by ICRC
- Eighty babies and 700 children
- Conclusion: less vulnerable than anticipated
- Current: Refugee population for Qatrom was 3,000 of the 5,000 capacity.

Repurposed Tent:
- Enormous bakery tent (10 m x 30 m) donated by the Turkish government
- Turkey to provide baking equipment.
- Train fourteen refugees to bake bread *(buka)*
- Bread to supply overflow of expected 6,000 refugees from Macedonia
- Guaranteed not to interfere with local bakery income
- Flood of refugees from Macedonia never materialized
- Baking equipment never arrived
- Tent repurposed as a community center

A Raft of Rumors:
- Spread like wildfire
- Caused unrest and agitation
- Warnings against recruitment of refugees to join the Kosovo Liberation Army (KLA) by my son, Will, Professor of Political Science, Florida State University
- Subtle pressure of duty to join the KLA while fighting in

Kosovo continued
- Mothers revealed to the medical staff that the KLA had taken their sons.
- Unsubstantiated talk of young girls being recruited reached management
- No solutions
- Constant worry

Abduction?
- A single man approached the RI tent at lunchtime
- The KLA took his sons at night and in secret
- Rumor now real
- Talk of recruitment in camp silenced.
- A suspected directive from Xhevat, the chairman of the refugee board
- Xhevat continued to be a challenge and agitator

NATO and Needs:
- Unified radio communication for all NGOs and agencies needed
- Evacuation plans and routes needed
- The British government agreed to fund the communication project
- British KFOR selected evacuation routes
- Qatrom helicopter pad, built by British KFOR, used to medivac sick and injured.

Influx of International Staff:
- Housing needed
- Local residents rented their homes at over inflated rates
- Augmented local income for homeowners
- The financial drain on the donor community
- US dollars and euros welcomed by local businesses
- The overabundance of international people without the expected refugees
- New camps empty

Incoming Refugees:
- RI the only camp in operation
- Refugees arrived from neighboring villages
- Refugees came from host families
- Busloads of refugees arrived from Macedonia
- RI welcomed all the Kosovar refugees

Salaries for Albanians:
- Competition between NGOs and agencies inflated salaries for drivers, interpreters, workers
- The prefekture and the local government finally set a salary policy
- A little too late, as employees jumped from one organization to another for a higher salary
- RI lost two employees
- UNHCR mandated all refugee worker volunteers without giving any special privileges.

Twilight settled over Qatrom as the ongoing concerns of camp management hung over me like a dark, ominous cloud. How to resolve these issues and quell the unrest—would the answers come? Too exhausted to think, I trundled home. I entered the office, and the scent of delicious hot food greeted me. My stomach growled. Ascending the stairs to our communal living quarters, I heard the laughter of my colleagues as they gathered around the dining table. Eager to join in, I let the somber thoughts evaporate, ready to participate in the shared camaraderie.

Refugee family in their tent

Hospitality amid Tragedy

Amid tragedy, loss, and heartache, gracious hospitality flowed from the women in Qatrom. Daily, the gentle, kind, and loving Kosovar women invited me into their tents for coffee and conversation. I could not accept most of the time, until one day when the warm, sunlit day lent a few minutes to relax and accept the invitation. Entering the tent, I saw a home that the mother had created in her cramped living space. Mattresses lined the tent's perimeter with meager belongings nestled in the corners. Her husband had carried all their possessions crammed into backpacks as the family trudged to safety. The layout created an open space in the center to sit for eating, conversation, and family time. Blankets, taut enough to bounce a coin, hugged the mattresses. The tent floor was spotless, without a trace of sand or dirt. My mind reeled. *How did she do it?*

 The mother blushed when I complimented her. She directed me to a spot on the floor and the rest of the family took their seats. The mother crouched near the tent opening, tending to a pot of boiling water over a one-burner propane flame canister. She prepared instant Turkish coffee in china cups from Kosovo. With a slight bow and a smile, she handed me a cup. She joined us after serving everyone. I welcomed the respite. We sat in perfect harmony, enjoying the peaceful atmosphere and each other's company. The feelings of love and appreciation flowed between us.

Sensing my time to leave, the mother, with a pleading, desperate look, placed her hand on my arm. Fear stared out at me as she began her story. Reliving the horror, the children trembled and clutched their parents. As she spoke, I saw images of anger and hatred in the eyes of the Serbian military with their AK47s, forcing this frightened family from their home. The acrid smell of smoke filled my nostrils; smoke burned my eyes. Shivers ran through me as she told how the soldiers threatened them with death if they did not move faster. Her words painted images of them at the edge of the village, and I could see their house burn to the ground in my mind's eye. My heart grew heavy. I saw visions of destruction, anger, and despair. Tears streamed down our faces. We embraced, clinging to each other for comfort and strength. Being present and listening with empathy was the only salve I had, although I longed to alleviate their pain and anguish. As we released each other, the mother said, "My mother was separated from us and is at the refugee camp in Kukes."

"The International Committee of the Red Cross reunites families," I said. "I will ask them to find your mother and bring her to Qatrom, although it may take time."

She threw her arms around me, held me tight, and whispered, "Bless you."

A week later, as I was preparing for another distribution, the daughter ran to me, shouting, my grandmother just arrived, and we are together as a family. I dropped everything. We embraced, danced up and down, and squealed with joy. Other staff members joined in the celebrate the reunion of a split family. Silently, I thanked ICRC for their work in reuniting families. I was forever changed after hearing the refugees' stories and witnessing their grief.

Fatigue

> *"Fatigue makes cowards of us all."*
> *- General George Patton*

As much as I loved hands-on fieldwork, exhaustion swooped in like an unwanted plague, numbing my mind and my body. I felt I could barely function. Twelve to fourteen-hour days, no breaks, and constant demands took its toll on me. Sunrise at 5 AM and barking dogs, chained to the roof of our neighbor, interrupted what little sleep I could get. The refugees and staff had severe head colds; everyone was cranky. Not in the best mood, I dressed and dragged myself to the 8 AM UNCHR meeting—two more busloads of refugees from Macedonia later today.

No separation between living quarters and the office, making work seem 24/7, added to the fatigue. Rumors floated from headquarters of another house, which would ease our cramped quarters. With the international staff, Albanian staff and office in the existing place, the thought of another home for the Albanian staff sounded ideal. Everyone would eat at the house for the International staff.

Fatigue ballooned minor issues into more considerable annoyances. Refugees and staff were equally cranky. So many people in such a small area accumulated a tremendous amount of trash, paper, litre sofa bottles, spoiled pampers, swept dirt from the tents, etc. *From where does it all come?* Trash bins in each cluster proved inadequate, with the bins overflowing and scattering debris everywhere. Unable to tolerate it, I grabbed large garbage bags and cleaned up the trash in one cluster. Soon, several young boys between nine and eleven joined me. I suggested making a game of who could collect the most trash. Giggles erupted as the boys surged about the camp, collecting items to stuff into the bags, often spilling back out in their haste—a mood changer, and I needed one, as their giggles and willingness to help touched my heart. They soon tired of the game, dumped the bags, and ran off chasing and poking at each other. *I appreciated the little help they gave me. It touched my heart to see them laughing and playing – a sign of their resilience.*

As the trash situation continued to mount, management met with the local authorities, called the Prefekture, to discuss additional garbage pickup. Resistant at first, the Prefekture agreed to collect the trash twice per week instead of once. Pleased with the decision, we left, leaving RI headquarters to negotiate the price. It pleased everyone, until the garbage trucks arrived at 6 AM, waking the refugees. Frustration reigned, as grumbling filtered into management's ears—the look and cleanliness of the camp improved, lessening the possibility of spreading disease and attracting rats. *I understand their frustration. No control over their food, living in tents, no electricity, pit latrines, and tent showers—a constant reminder of their hardships and trauma of losing loved ones and being forced from their beloved homeland. At least I could go to a house with intermittent water and electricity, flushing toilets, and bathtubs.*

Another daily annoyance occurred around food. The Salvation Army prepared lunch and dinner for the refugees. Cooking tents scattered throughout the camp. Volunteers from the refugee population helped prepare and distribute the food. The smells of food cooking wafted through the Qatrom, causing empty stomachs to rumble. Long lines formed during feeding hours. Impatient refugees restored to grumbling as their children ran wild, weaving in and out of lines, poking at their siblings, which caused screams and laughter. Waves of complaints about the inconvenience of the lines and the food quality filled the air at each feeding. The staple of meat and bread did not exist as it did at home. Meals comprising of beans and rice with occasional canned meat didn't satisfy. A local restaurant delivered gyros and cold drinks for the RI staff to the site at noon — no variety, day after day, the same food. I understood the frustration of the refugees. *My heart goes out to these beautiful people, who had to change so much to be alive. Everything in their lives had turned upside down. I know I would bitch and moan to someone.*

Still dragging for fatigue, three railroad boxcar containers arrived unannounced. Answered prayers. Lunch half-eaten, everyone pitched in to move the materials into the safety of lockable containers, which reduced theft. The German Red Crescent erected the new massive (ten meters by thirty meters) distribution and registration tent next to the boxcar containers. Fatigue lifted. The day seemed brighter. New refugees arrived at 3:30 PM. By 5 PM we completed the registration, distribution and tent assignments, allowing time for us to attend the British KFOR meeting — a time to relax and let go.

Evening Break

Before the evening break, sixty-six refugees arrived, including a man in a wheelchair with his wife and child. What to do with a disabled person? Qatrom could not accommodate a wheelchair. We scrambled to find a temporary solution. The best we could do was a tent near the pit latrine and shower. I radioed Marci. She contacted Handicap International in Tirana to plan for a transfer. Luckily, they found a place in Korçë that could take the family the following day.

One problem solved. But then, just as we were about to leave, a UNHCR helicopter arrived with six bundles of blankets, which needed to be stored. All finished, we went home for dinner.

After dinner, a small group of staff strolled along the tree-lined streets to taste the local beer and listen to music at an outdoor pub. Away from the dirt road and vendor stalls, tree-lined streets and small parks dotted the landscape. At dusk, the police cordoned off the paved streets to become pedestrian walkways during the spring and summer months. As the golden light of the day faded and the fragrant smell of blossoming trees and flowers filled the air, the local families emerged to stroll and enjoy the warm spring evening. Many pushed baby carriages, while the older children skipped alongside; their lilting voices filled the air with happiness and delight. *The normalcy and sincerity of the scene was a welcomed respite from the stress of the camp — a true delight to enjoy the sights and sounds of a blissful spring evening with colleagues.*

One Albanian staff accompanied me wherever I went. Not only to interpret for me, but to offer protection, as UNHCR warned us not to walk anywhere alone, especially at night. Eight of us sat on white plastic chairs around a long wooden table covered with a white paper tablecloth. Shortly, pitchers of *Korçë Bierre* and plastic cups arrived. The cold beer and cool breeze swept away the tension and fatigue of the day. Music and laughter filled the air as stories of the day erupted from us. I marveled at the camaraderie and tight bonds formed in such a short time. It had been a mere two weeks. I delighted being with the Albanian staff and asking them questions about their lives and their dreams. One of my favorite questions was: "If you had a magic wand, what would your life look like?"

Most repeated the same answer, although expressed differently. They wanted suitable, steady employment, marriage and the ability to support their families while living in peace — such a universal desire. It warmed my heart. I loved these encounters as I learned more about the universal oneness in us all.

The magic of the evening ended around 9 PM as we sauntered back to the house, feeling relaxed and refreshed, with promises made to do this more often.

Meeting at the Prefekture

Marci and I, as managers of Qatrom, gathered at the prefekture with the UNHCR representative and others to discuss issues and programs involving the refugees in Korçë.

"I must inform you that at 1:00 AM on the Bulevard Republica, a grenade exploded and there were shots fired from an AK47. One person was killed and the situation had been not resolved," said the prefekt. "Please do not walk at night."

Marci and I looked at each other with concern. The event happened in the square near where we held the morning briefings. We heard rumors about organized crime in the area—in addition to the refugees, we now had to worry about criminals?

"In addition," he informed us, "the prime minister of Albania will arrive at Qatrom at 9:30 AM to meet with the NGOs working in the camp." Surprised, Marci and I rolled our eyes at each other—how nice to give us ample warning.

We told the prefekt and the UNHCR representative that a riot nearly erupted the previous day because of the issues and discontent over the quality and quantity of bread. We met with three refugee committee members to discuss solutions. They told me that the board chairman did little to quell the agitation. I said that I would speak to him about his role as a leader.

"The committee wants the bakery and delivery changed," I said. "We also heard from the WFP representative that they require a 24-hour advanced notice to prepare the yeast and flour mixture for the correct number of loaves."

"As for another matter, are there Pampers available? If not, could UNHCR request Pampers from other organizations working in Korçë? We were running low in Qatrom." We had counted the number of babies born in 1997, 1998, and 1999 to determine the number of Pampers needed.

We also discussed that the representative from Dorkas took 900 unused mattresses and delivered lice shampoo to Medicos del Mundos. There was the question as to why sixty-six refugees arrived at Qatrom from Duval camp? And the Salvation Army told us that they discovered pork in the donated canned food and bacon drippings in the bags of potato chips. Since the Muslim refugees did not eat pork as part of their religion, they decided to eliminate the items before they arrived to avoid any misconceptions.

Before we adjourned, the UNHCR representative ended the meeting on a happy note with the news that a refugee from Qatrom had reunited with his family at the refugee camp in Kukes. After saying goodbye, Marci and I rushed back to Qatrom to prepare for the Albanian prime minister's visit. Excitement rippled through the camp with the news, and the refugees gathered near the gate to greet him.

Complaints

Complain, complain, complain—day after day, complaints on top of complaints with few solutions bombarded me. There were very rarely easy solutions. Being a mother and a nurturing person, I was frustrated at the inability to make life a little easier for them. Most protests were ongoing—some we could solve, others we could not.

Bread, or *buka,* was a constant problem in Qatrom. It was a staple of the Kosovar Albanian diet. One morning, as the refugees lined up at the Salvation Army feeding tents for breakfast, they learned the *buka* was unavailable. The crowd shouted and screamed at the Salvation Army staff, causing a near riot. Xhevat, a lawyer from Pristina and the elected community board leader, entered the fray. Xhevat, thin-lipped and unsmiling eyes, commanded attention. He did not want to be a refugee in Qatrom and challenged everything—my nemesis. Dressed in his tracksuit, he jumped on a table with a bull horn and incited the crowd further rather than calming the situation. Marci and I arrived after the UNCHR morning briefing with Xhilda, Elton, Genti, and Indrit. We were greeted at the compound gate by agitated refugee leaders.

As they relayed the morning's events, I realized it was a

delivery and a problem of quantity and quality, which would haunt us throughout the coming months. We needed an immediate solution. There were other food complaints. The refugees received two cans of herring per week and eggs or cheese each day. They wanted meat, fresh vegetables, and more bread. Quality remained an issue, although the refugees were getting more than the World Food Program (WFP) standard amount. The RI staff learned two-burner propane portable stoves had been donated but had not yet arrived. That there was only one stove per cluster created further headaches, arguments, and complaints.

Lack of hot water was another constant complaint, especially from the women. Showering in a tent with cold water, a bucket, and a cup appealed to no one. Having worked in the area for many years, a woman staff member from Dorkas explained that the underlying complaint was cultural. The women needed to wash after having sexual relations, a practice they referred to as needing to wash their hair. Never in a million years would I have been able to discern that meaning. We muddled through as best we could by listening and trying to resolve their issues. The water would be warmer with longer, warmer days, since the pipes were under the sandy soil, which heated as the sun beat down on the ground. It was a slight consolation, considering they would never have hot water in the camp unless they boiled the water.

Around 2 PM, the gates scrapped open, and a police car sped into Qatrom. Dust flew as the vehicle screeched to a halt in front of the RI compound. From inside the tent, we could hear angry voices and refugees running to witness the proceedings. Xhilda and I bolted from the tent to investigate. A police officer charged toward us. Holding my hands up as we approached the police officer, I instructed Xhilda to translate word for word when I spoke with him. One of our refugees and a local man were in the police car. Refugees strained to hear and surrounded the police vehicle.

I demanded the refugee be released. The young man was under the protection of UNHCR. The young man leapt from the car and disappeared into the crowd as though the group swallowed him. Xhilda and I could not believe our eyes. How could anyone disappear into thin air? Unhappy, the police and local man left.

I hugged Xhilda and said, "I couldn't be prouder of you. You translated with composure and never wavered. You looked the police officer straight in the eye. Thank you."

She said, "I shook with fear."

"My knees trembled, also, but we were within our rights, which make us strong."

What would my attitude be if I had been driven from my home, seeing my house destroyed, loved ones raped or killed, forced to live in a tent, eat food I didn't like, use pit latrines and cold showers? Would I complain? I thought so much of their lives was no longer in their control that complaining was the one thing they could control, so I listened and addressed what I could.

All Work and No Play

Body language of the Albania staff manifested in late arrivals, lack of enthusiasm, dull eyes, few smiles and peppered with biting, sarcastic comments—symptoms of working 12-14 hours per day for twelve days straight without a break. Action needed. Always short staffed, management devised a plan to schedule breaks on a rotational basis. Today, the first staff member returned to his home in Tirana for a two-day break. Upon his return, another member left. The International staff, unable to leave the area, created a plan to rotate half-days off. Attitudes shifted, enthusiasm and dedication returned—the miracle of simple fixes. Pride swelled within me as I marveled at the resilience of our bare bones staff.

At the morning briefing, UNHCR awarded Relief International to manage the future second German-built camp. Answered prayers came with the arrival of a new volunteer from the U.S. Under my tutelage, Joanne learned camp management, Relief International-style. Besides, she managed the data spreadsheet to track the number of refugees in Qatrom: name, age, date of arrival home village and tent location—a task delegated to me but dropped through the cracks with no time. Relief and gratitude swept over me with her willingness to tackle this necessary task. Moreover, her computer skills far exceeded mine. With the anticipation of more refugees flooding into the area, RI started recruiting for additional staff. For a rich and rewarding opportunity of a lifetime, please apply to Relief International, Los Angeles, CA.

Three Unexpected Gifts

What is a gift? A gift is something you give or receive from someone, or a natural ability or talent. Lady Luck shined down on Qatrom on 17 May. We received unexpected gifts, which were the best kind.

The first gift: Morning prayers at 4:45 AM interrupted my dream of sandy beaches, blue-green ocean waves, and the sweet scent of saltwater as a gentle breeze kissed my face. After a quick breakfast and my chilled water bottle, I entered the RI management tent and stubbed my toe on a stack of cartons. *Ouch!* Where did these boxes come from? The packages contained books of the Koran, which appeared with no note to indicate who donated or delivered them. Uncertain of what to do, I contacted the refugee board and asked them to distribute the books to the refugees. Xhevat, the Board Chairman, gave me a fascinating history lesson of the region.

He said, "Ten to twelve generations ago, my ancestors were all Catholic until the Ottoman Empire conquered the area. The Ottoman rulers gave my ancestors a choice to remain Catholic and pay taxes or convert to Islam and pay no taxes. They became Muslims, although we in Kosovo loosely practice the religion."

"No wonder they converted," I said. "Thank you for explaining that."

The second gift: Fairy dust continued to sprinkle over Qatrom. Care International, an NGO, replaced Dorkas, a Dutch NGO, in delivering the bread. Previously, the bread issue nearly caused a riot. Being a staple in the Kosovar Albanian diet, the designated half loaf of bread created tensions among the refugees. The Salvation Army, the refugee food committee, and I negotiated to increase the bread delivery by 23% more bread, having 123 loaves delivered instead of 100. Unfortunately, the information didn't reach the refugee population; thus, the agitation remained high. Food complaints lurked in the background, a kind of perpetual white noise.

The third gift: At 2:00 PM, Lady Luck blessed us again. With supplies dangerously low, a tailor truck the size of a flatbed truck lumbered into camp, carrying supplies. The miracle of timing. Once the semi parked, a steady stream of Pampers, disinfectant for the pit latrines, bathing soap and shampoo, and laundry detergent rolled from the truck into our lockable storage containers. The materials arrived in time for distribution the following day. I breathed a sigh of relief and thanked the driver—his timing was perfect. I offered a silent prayer of thanks to the Polish government. (I learned later from my cousin, who lived in Germany and was listening to the Polish news, saw me being interviewed as we unloaded the truck. She shrieked for her husband to come and watch. She told me I spoke perfect Polish).

Bobbie with children

Refugee children filling water bottles

Children at Play

The sun beat down on Qatrom with unrelenting heat. I plodded along the dirt road with my head down and shoulders rounded, weighted down with fatigue and worry. Sweat dripped down my face, stinging my eyes, and my clothes clung to my body as I worked my way to the RI compound.

Squeals of delight and gleeful giggles broke my concentration. I approached one of the water taps and saw five boys, ages five to seven, fill liter-sized plastic soda bottles with water. They hurled the water, which flew in every direction, soaking each other and turning the dirt to mud around them. On impulse, my mischievous inner child engulfed me. I rushed to the tap, cupped my hands with water, and splashed the nearest boy. Surprised and cautious, he and the other boys included me in their water battle, the water cooling my hot skin. The fun began. I darted between the boys as they doused me with water. Laughter filled the air as we indulged in a game of chase, water flying everywhere.

Harried mothers charged from their tents, screaming, *"Jo!!"* The boys stopped in their tracks. Knowing only a few phrases in Albanian, I understood, *No!* I knew the mothers were scolding their sons with loud, harsh tongue lashings.

I raised my hands and said, "*Më fal* [forgive me], gesturing to myself that it was my fault. *Un jam gjyshe. Argëtim. Faleminderit.*" [I am a grandmother. Fun. Thank you.]

The mothers nodded at me while their eyes stayed riveted on their boys. Softening, they smiled and said, "*Faleminderit.*"

I bent down to the boys, "*Faleminderit, argëtim.*" The fun was over for me, and I said, "*Lamtumirë* [goodbye]."

Wet, I continued my way with a lighter heart, a broader smile, and a spring in my step. I felt ready to tackle whatever would come next. A bit of silliness was just what I needed. (My few words and phrases in Albanian connected me with the refugee community; they appreciated my effort and rewarded me with their warmth). "A little nonsense now and then is cherished by the wisest men." - Roald Dahl.

The laughter of children released a frequency deep within me, spreading contentment and joy throughout my body, mind, emotions. I often just stood and watched, basking in the joy of the children's laughter, feeling renewed, inspired, and revitalized. Thank you for the gift of laughter—it heals the spirit of all who hear and all who take part.

To quote Stuart Brown, MD, "Play energizes and enlivens us. It eases our burdens. It renews our natural sense of optimism and opens us up to new possibilities."

What do children do when there are no toys? So many questions popped into my mind. Why is there never time to search for answers and solutions? Sometimes answers came while I walked down the wide dirt road that divided Qatrom in half. I watched in wonder at the children's ingenuity to create objects with which to play. Young boys covered their heads with empty cardboard boxes. Smaller boxes served as swords and they adopted the stance of fencing players and shouted, "On-guard." They thrust and parried as their imagination turned boxes into fencing foils. Soon, the larger cartons fell to the ground as they maneuvered their small makeshift swords. Giggles erupted. Cartons flew in all directions. After retrieving the boxes, the dueling began again until they tired of the game. They picked up the boxes and returned to their tents to find another game. The expended energy of play released some of the traumatic memories.

With their parents' help, they made pinwheels by cutting blades from plastic bottles and attaching them to sticks. The pinwheels swirled around in the wind or when the children ran to create the current. *From where did the wire to attach the blades come — perhaps the local vendors?* I never found out. I saw toy cars made from plastic bottles and scraps of wire. For the younger children, parents attached strings to the makeshift cars, turning them into pull toys; ingenuity at work — marvelous.

One morning, staff found several unoccupied tents flat on the ground minus the tent ropes and poles. Curious and suspicious, we walked around Qatrom to investigate. Noise led us to Sections B and C. The refugees had erected a volleyball net made from the tent ropes and there was a competitive game in progress. Children cheered and waited in the wings to rotate into the game — camera time. Smiling with my face and heart, I captured a snapshot of the ball in mid-air before returning to the compound. Since the number of expected refugees never arrived in Qatrom, we let the volleyball net stand. We also chose not to inform RI headquarters in Tirana. That afternoon, I told the board that management left the volleyball net up, but they must ensure no other nets appeared. They agreed.

Further along the dirt road, I saw two swings. Squeals of delight erupted as girls pumped their legs to see how high they could go — ah, the other collapsed tent poles and ropes. The smiles on their faces acted as a balm for them and me. If there had not been a line of children waiting for their turn, I would have asked if I could join in the fun on the swing. Seeing the children happy and playing showed a sign of normalcy.

On windy days, we witnessed boys of all ages flying homemade kites in the fields next to Qatrom. Dads stood ready to help untangle kites and to get them airborne after a nosedive. I welcomed the rare sight of seeing fathers and sons in joint activity.

Mindy, the therapist from New York, designed scavenger hunts for the children of all ages three afternoons each week. Like clockwork, the children would gather around her like puppies waiting for a treat. I did not know where she found items to hide or the creative places to hide them. The clamoring of voices showed excitement and success. Mindy rewarded all the children with big hugs.

Sabri, the educational coordinator, conducted several track and field events for the other children after their studies. Relay races, soccer games, tug of war, kickball, to name a few activities. Teachers and parents gathered as referees and cheerleaders.

I marveled at the creativity of the children, parents, teachers, and staff, who created toys and activities to entertain the children with ages ranging from infant to 15 and older. I witnessed the benefits of creativity and play, reinforcing the necessity to find time for both. George Bernard Shaw wrote, "We don't stop playing because we grow old; we grow old because we stop playing." Or in the words of Pooh Bear, "When life throws you a rainy day, play in puddles." It reminded me what fun it was to play in puddles and the joy I found when I watched my two sons splash around in puddles and slush when they were young.

A Gentle Giant

Tall, slender, and handsome, Sabri stood out among the refugees. He was the educational coordinator in Qatrom. A gentle giant, not in stature, but in his calm and commanding demeanor. An engineer by trade, he devised plans to organize activities for the children from morning until noon. He cared deeply for the children, their education, and their well-being, even though he was unmarried and had no children of his own. And he understood that focusing on studies would help to alleviate their trauma.

Crowds of children surrounded him as if he were the Pied Piper. He organized classes and chose adults to teach a variety of subjects, including English. Thirty-meter by ten-meter tents were partitioned into many "classrooms" — plus two small stand-alone tents. Relief International hired an educational specialist to work alongside the camp educators. Afternoons held physical activity and games. Under Sabri's direction and tutelage, the education of the children thrived.

One afternoon, I stopped Sabri and asked, "Would it be possible for the children to communicate with children from the USA? It would provide a wonderful opportunity for cross-cultural understanding."

His eyes lit up as he replied, "Wonderful, I will ask the children." He walked away with a spring in his step.

Within a few days, Sabri handed me his letter. I found an American who worked in Korçë and spoke fluent Albanian to translate his message. I found a quiet corner in the RI tent and read. Tears streamed down my face as his words pierced my heart. Soon, the staff entered. Concern crossed their faces as they rushed to me, asking, "Are you okay?"

Unable to speak, I nodded and handed them the letter. They read it and we clung together and cried, delving into a more profound understanding of these beautiful people's pain and suffering.

The letter read: "Warm greetings from a man from the burned land (Kosovo) and greetings from thousands of kids without families, without homes, without parental affection. In the name of the truth, I am writing of the valuable word, in the name of the human love that keeps the world alive.

Even that I don't know you, because I have never seen you and I can't imagine how you look like, but I know for sure that you are a human being made of meat and blood. We are similar creatures, but we are different because you are in your homeland, have a house, and are not dependent upon somebody's desire to give you a piece of bread. You've never seen the corpses of your dears and passing over them. I don't know if you have children or not, but if you have, I guess they are happy and quiet, and nobody dares to disturb their dreams. If you have three or four children, I have 1,000 of them to whom I can only give frozen smiles and pats that hopefully help them forget their traumatic moments and the war. I am trying to be their mother and father, their brother and sister, their toy and dream, their bed, their song which embraces them and puts them to sleep as their mothers would do. Maybe it is, but I'm the second family for all of them, as you are for your family. But I would like to emphasize your valuable assistance, which motivates us to work. I'm one of the Kosovars of this camp that takes care of entertainment for those traumatized children. That is why I decided to write you this letter about our work in Korçë (Albania). When I see your people caring for us, I am deeply touched and thought that you are better people than our good people are. Hoping this letter includes all the gratefulness of our suffered people, I would like to send you my best regards. - Children Educational Coordinator Qatrom (Refugee) Camp, Korçë, Albania."

Although Sabri carried a heavy burden on his shoulders, he never wavered in his dedication to the comfort and well-being of the children. He remained a guiding light for the traumatized children, a pillar of strength in a time of chaos, an inspiration, and a hero to all of us in Qatrom—a gentle giant.

I filed the letters away, not forgotten, but to surface another day in the perfect format, as the intended cross-cultural exchange never came to fruition—time and the language barrier didn't work.

United States Delegation

A promise of rain hung over Qatrom. The stifling air remained still. Without a breeze, the heat in the tents amplified. There was no relief from the torrid, relentless sun.

At 10:00 AM, a delegation from the U.S. Department of State arrived unannounced. I scrambled to assemble the RI staff for a briefing. Everyone gathered in the RI tent. One delegate asked, "What are the number and flow of refugees from Macedonia?"

"All the details of refugees come from UNHCR. We have no direct contact with Macedonia. We just learned that UNCHR received a fax from the Macedonian government stating a convoy of 500 refugees would be transported to Qatrom on the 21st of May. Sometimes busloads of refugees arrive unannounced. When that happens, we must scramble to get them registered and settled," I said.

Another delegate said, "The intense fighting in Kosovo continues. An additional 100,000 Kosovar Albanians fled to Macedonia. That number created a pressure point at the Kosovo/Macedonian border, known as no-man's-land, with no facilities to accommodate the refugees. Problems continue in Kukes. Last week gangs entered the camp, sold drugs and grabbed young girls for prostitution and sex slaves."

"The news filtered into Qatrom, causing heightened anxiety and fear among the refugees. I'll bring it up with the community leaders. We have already had one break-in at night by the local Albanians," I said.

After the delegation left, I met with the community leaders, who created patrols to roam the camp from dust until dawn. Next, I contacted Gerard F., the head of the UNCHR office in Korçë, who promised to inform the prefekt and the local police of the potential threat.

Relief International hired an unarmed private security agency from 8:00 PM to 6 AM to guard the entrance and stored materials. Neither the local police nor the prefekt wanted firearms in Qatrom. RI management did not wish to have armed guards either — tension and unrest remained high and could explode like a powder keg at any moment.

The day ended with clouds blowing in and releasing a gentle, refreshing rain while the sweet smell of petrichor filled the air. The droplets calmed the dust and dirt and cooled the atmosphere. It was a welcome relief to us. I wondered if it had the same effect on the refugees.

Medicos del Mundo, Spain

Medicos del Mondo, Spain (MDM), provided medical care at Qatrom. Each day, the MDM tents filled with refugees, forming long lines with no place to sit except on the ground to wait their turn. Complaints consisted of diarrhea, lice, scabies, upper respiratory ailments, and other infirmities. A dedicated tent for female issues stood beside the medical tent for women to discuss trauma, fear, children, STDs, and rape. The clinic opened at 8 AM and closed at 7 PM daily. An Albanian doctor from Korçë covered during the night. An ambulance was available on a 24-hour basis to medivac refugees. MDM asked for a list of refugee midwives to assist when needed.

As the relentless rays of the sun beat down on the refugees and dry dirt from the road swirled in the air, the need for shade accelerated. As the temperatures soared, MDM requested baseball caps and sunscreen. More and more refugees complained of sunburn and headaches with no shade, except for the one tree at the entrance of Qatrom. I wrote a proposal to UNHCR to provide one plastic sheeting per tent for shading. Once the tarps arrived, the white and blue plastic sheeting with the UNHCR logo dotted the landscape. The awnings sprang to life and provided much-needed shade outside the tent openings.

MDM reported that since the basic needs of the refugees had been met, they would conduct a needs assessment regarding psycho-social problems, like anxiety, depression, and insomnia. Tending to the physical and emotional needs demanded constant attention, yet in contrast to the trauma, our camp witnessed the miracles of birth and hope. Lucky stars hovered above Qatrom as MDM, and a local midwife delivered the first newborn refugee baby. Celebration was the order of the day. Staff arrived at camp to learn both mother and baby were well. I pondered in awe: how did an eight-month pregnant woman trudge over a mountain in the cold and snow, land in a refugee camp, and deliver a healthy baby?

 Few women gathered in the camp, seen only walking their children or gathering by the water taps. They spent most of their time caring for their families. Crouched down with their skirts pulled over their legs and hair hidden with a head covering, women squeezed between the tent tie-downs to scrub their clothes in cold water using only a small basin and a bucket of water retrieved from the communal water taps. Articles of clothing waved a friendly greeting from the tent lines. Even simple tasks took hours of arduous work, all to ensure their families had clean clothes and tidy homes. While walking through the camp, articles of clothing waved a friendly greeting from the tent lines. Cleaning, laundry, and caring for their family occupied their time. Harsh conditions dwindled at the feet of the mighty spirit of these women.

After another busy day, I did not think of management meetings or weekly status reports due to RI headquarters in Tirana. I did not stress about the oversight of things like food and supplies, water, and sanitation. I thought about the miracle of birth and hope, about the refugee women, themselves miraculous in so many ways.

School Dilemma

*A*t 2:00 PM, another surprise visit interrupted the activities of Qatrom. The local head of education for the district of Korçë and three local Albanian teachers arrived unannounced. They wanted to meet with the RI staff and Sabri, the coordinator of children's activities. They requested that the refugee children attend the local school for the summer session. Sabri and the RI staff were reluctant, causing the local teachers to become more agitated. Everyone spoke at once, and no one listened. The debate reverted to Albanian, leaving the interpreters silent and me puzzled. I had the false impression the Albanian teachers would serve as trainers for the acting refugee teachers; thus, I did not understand the forceful insistence of the refugee children to attend the local school. The more heated the discussion, the more suspicious I became. Although I did not understand the words, the anger, tone, and aggressive body language spoke volumes. My gut screamed a hidden agenda lurked underneath the surface. I stood, held up my hand, and said, "The most important factor is the children's safety and well-being." I repeated this sentiment so often that I sounded like a broken record.

I learned the provincial government thought the refugee

children would receive a better in camp than the local schools. The parents communicated their fears regarding their children leaving the camp and their wish to have them remain in Qatrom. Given these factors, I needed to understand the real agenda. I suspected that the disagreement had nothing to do with the children, but was a political move for the local educational team. With the temperature in the room rising, I stood again and said, "This discussion is finished. The RI staff, parents, children, and Sabri will convene at the local school in an hour. Now everyone must leave."

The parents, their children, Sabri, Elton, and I gathered to walk a half hour to the school. Whispering to Elton, I said, "There is something beneath the local school committee's anger and insistence. I need to understand the hidden agenda to make the correct decision since my only concern is the safety of the children. I am inclined to say no, so I need verification. Will you help me?"

Elton said, "I will see what I can find out."

Upon arrival at the school, I was impressed. Each room contained a row of tables and benches with two students per table, plus a heater for cold winter days. Once everyone crammed into the classroom, the discussion soon accelerated into a yelling match. Teachers and parents screamed at each other. Again, I observed from the sidelines. Seeing no progress, I pounded the table, stood with my arm raised, and in a firm voice, said, "Enough. Our only concern is for the health and safety of the refugee children—nothing else matters. Discussion finished! I need the local committee to submit a proposal and present it to the refugees. Do not include younger children because the walking distance is too far. Thank you for your time." I turned to the headmaster and said, "There is no need to shout. Diplomacy is always the best way to resolve issues."

He replied, "I know nothing about diplomacy, and the teachers always speak in loud voices. Please come for coffee on Monday."

On the walk back to camp, Elton confirmed my suspicions. He said, "An outside Muslim organization will refurbish the school and increase the salaries of all the teachers and administrators if the refugee children attend the school."

That did it for me. Decision made—the children would remain in Qatrom. End of the discussion. I would inform the headmaster on Monday. I told the parents and Sabri of my decision. They smiled with relief. Many parents embraced me with grateful hugs and murmurs of thank you. A satisfying feeling settled in my stomach with the knowledge I had made the correct decision.

Leisure Time

The young staff would go out at night as the days became longer. I relished the quiet time by myself—a time to read, write emails or relax, often falling fast asleep while reading. One balmy late spring evening as dusk slowly approached, I joined the Albanian staff for a beer, conversation, and dancing at a local pub. While Elton and I danced, beer bottles flew and smashed on the stage, broken glass flying everywhere. The more we danced, the more beer bottles flew. Baffled and anxious, I stopped dancing, ready to bolt. Over the loud music of the outdoor café, I shouted, "Elton, what is happening?"

With a wide grin on his face, he told me that the crowd was happy and excited to see a foreigner dance with a local, a strange custom. I bolted off the dance floor—not my kind of fun.

On the walk back to the house, I asked Elton to tell me about his family.

Before answering, Elton looked off in the distance. A shadow of sadness crossed his face. In a halting voice, as his eyes filled with tears, he said, "My parents won the lottery to immigrate to the United States. My younger brother went with them. I couldn't go because I was older than eighteen. Now I stay in our empty house. I miss them. I don't know when I will see them again, although we talk on the telephone from time to time."

"Oh, Elton, I did not know. My heart aches for you. I know the separation is painful. I am separated from my family, but I know I can return. Do you have other family members in Tirana?"

"Yes, I have my grandmother, aunts, uncles, and cousins," he said, "but it is not the same."

I nodded. We returned to the house in silence, each of us wrapped in our own thoughts. I pondered the pain of separation from family and longing to reunite; the recognition deepened my empathy for the refugees in our care.

Besides an occasional evening at a local outdoor pub, one restaurant in town opened its doors to the international community for cocktails and hors d'oeuvres on Wednesdays. The restaurant offered a respite, as it provided us with a sense of community, since all international workers spoke English, no matter their country of origin. Relying on interpreters through the day created stress and fatigue. At times, I wanted to scream and cover my ears to turn the language off. Everyone smiled and indulged in my attempts to speak their language. Stifled giggles filled the air when I used a wrong word, indicting I said something I shouldn't have. Ah, the joys of language. My admiration grew daily as I imagined how my interpreters may have found speaking another language exhausting, too. They never complained, at least not to me.

Inspection by Kosovar Refugees

A make-or-break day for Qatrom—a delegation of twenty Kosovar refugees staying in Macedonia arrived before noon for a tour. The group wanted to inspect our facilities to determine if they should move here. UNHCR extolled Qatrom as a model camp and planned to emulate the structure in additional camps in Korçë, thus, today's visit. I acted as a tour guide. The group included the visiting refugees and some of our refugee committee members. As we toured the facilities and activities, the delegation asked thoughtful and provocative questions. Not speaking the language, I could tell the interaction was excellent by the smiles, nodding of heads, and the smooth flow of the discourse. Xhevat joined us in praising the camp, RI staff, and children's activities. The tour went well, so I thought, as I left the group and they departed for the buses to return to Macedonia.

In an instant, the illusion imploded. Outside Qatrom, journalists met to speak to the refugees. Xhevat criticized Qatrom and staff management in front of this captive audience, advising the refugee delegation to stay in Macedonia. I learned of this deception when my stunned interpreters told me what had happened. We assembled in the RI tent to discuss the two-faced comments of Xhevat, who continued to be a thorn in my side. He would say what he thought I wanted to hear, then do an about-face to cause unrest and discontent. I experienced this before during the bread incident when he agitated the crowd. I had to speak to Xhevat before the next committee meeting—perhaps a unique project could focus his attention away from dissent? Genti would be the best interpreter to help with the translation. He had a calm way of presenting thorny subjects to the refugees. Otherwise, I suspected Xhevat would continue to agitate.

After the delegation's episode, one of the committee members came into the RI tent. He said to me, "I plan to transfer from Qatrom to Pogradec today as soon as I collect my belongings."

Pogradec was a Greek refugee camp in an adjacent town. I asked, "Why?"

"I have been bothered by some refugees, so I have to leave." He refused to elaborate.

"I hate to see you go. You have been such an outstanding leader on the committee. I have enjoyed working with you, and I will miss you."

We embraced. Tears sprang from my eyes when he left to gather his belongings.

What caused him to take off? Did his leadership threaten others? Did tribal bickering get to him, creating tension and forcing him to flee? Saddened, I would never know. I could only speculate. Unanswered questions preyed upon me, but I had only brief moments to ponder them before other demands grabbed my attention.

War Crimes and an RI Officer

Sunbeams danced in the puddles left by rain from the night before. A refreshing breeze cooled the air, the humidity dropped, and the leaves stirred. The scent of fresh grass and flowers wafted in the air—all promises of a good day.

Without prior notice, a team from the U.S. Department of State entered Qatrom at 9 AM to collect evidence of human rights violation by Slobodan Milošević, the Serbian president of the Republic of Yugoslavia (1997-2000). The evidence was to be presented to the International Court of Justice in The Hague, Netherlands. Caught by surprise, I neglected to have the refugee board forewarn the refugees of the purpose of the visit. I said to the delegation, "The Refugee Board has to set guidelines to ensure the refugees' comfort and safety, and they need a promise from the Department of State that no reprisals will be made for their honesty before any interviews."

We met with the refugee board, who agreed to assist but declined the Department of State's suggestion of a central location for the interviews and required a committee member and a translator to be present at all meetings. The discussions, which would last several days, had to include willing participants without coercion. Once all agreed, the interview process began. However, the purpose of their presence did not get conveyed clearly through the refugee population, and the lapse in communication caused havoc as official-looking people created suspicion among the refugees. Disturbing rumors of Serbian journalists spread like wildfire and frightened the refugees. The medical staff from MDM reported the rumors to RI staff. I immediately called a board meeting and told them to gather the other refugee committee members to inform their sections of what was going on and asked for any volunteers to come forth with their stories. If I had thought to do this as soon as the State Department delegation arrived, I could have averted anxiety, suspicion, and rumors. I would not make that mistake again.

Later in the afternoon, Jeff, CFO from RI headquarters in Los Angeles, arrived to finalize the office setup and negotiate a separate house for the Albanian staff. He hired a local merchant to make gyro sandwiches for the staff lunches. Jeff and I had worked at the same refugee camp in Kenya, although at different times. We enjoyed an understanding and mutual bond. I asked Jeff to speak to the Refugee Board Chairman, Xhevat, regarding his duplicity and tendency to create tension rather than calm. Jeff talked to Xhevat using Xhevat's interpreter, who proved inadequate. Jeff put the chairman on notice, which prompted the interpreter to ask, "Will the chairman be replaced?"

Jeff replied, "I cannot dictate that. The board must decide."

Jeff and I were afraid Xhevat might intimidate the other board members who would not ask him to step down. We discussed the possibility of giving Xhevat an individual assignment to occupy his time. As a lawyer, Xhevat knew legal terms, rules, and regulations.

Before dinner, I found Xhevat and asked, "Would you be willing to draft a document with rules and regulations for running the Qatrom? I am sure someone in the office would type the document for you."

Xhevat replied, "I will draft something if I can have a picnic table at my tent so I can write."

"I can arrange that. Why don't you find someone to help you

carry it to your tent this evening so you can get started?"

Xhevat, always in need of recognition and prestige, would be the only one in camp to have a table at his tent. I smiled as I turned away.

In the Words of Children

A memorable day for the children's concert—the camp buzzed with excitement and activity. Dorcas had loaned us microphones, amplifiers, and a stage for the event. I invited UNHCR, NATO, all the local NGOs, and some of the local officials. Preparations began early in the morning for a 4 PM performance.

The children began by singing the Kosovar National Anthem. Then the master of ceremonies introduced each child, who read a poem or a composition that they had written. Themes of anger, bitterness, bombs, dead bodies, and burning houses dominated. Many spoke of their mother's blood being spilled on the earth. One third-grade girl delivered a poem about her empty school. A second-grade boy read his poem honoring his father and brothers who remained in Kosovo to fight for freedom. He expressed how much he missed them and wondered if they were still alive. At the end of his reading, someone from the audience presented him with an armband of the KLA. The audience erupted with cheers and tears. Lost innocence with rape, killing, burning, and bayonets—the words of seven-, eight-, nine-, and ten-year-old children rang in our ears. One eighth grader read a poem devoted to the KLA. The anger abated as the older children read their compositions — many comprised of hope, freedom, and the return to a free Kosovo.

The spirit of unity permeated the audience. We listened with heavy hearts to the trauma, suffering, and pain these children endured. The performers thanked the Albanians for so warmly accepting them into their country. The stories were raw and painful. They stood on their own as a testament to the brutality of war.

What follows is a sample of those stories. A friend translated the following letters in the children's word without edits.

"Hello, I am a student in 7th grade in Prishtina. You have certainly heard about the terrible war and the bloodletting that Serbia has been doing since March 1998 against my people, defenseless…Serbia has made a war that is dirty and without meaning — wiping out, burning, stealing, that is, plundering and kicking out my people. I now am one of those people that have been kicked out with violence from Kosova. I think it is after a terrible journey of ten days; I am in the fields of Korçë, a city here in Albania.

My loving friends, now I do not want to burden you down with our sufferings and pain with the disappearance of joy and smiles from our charred lips, but I want to deliver this message to you and to all the children who love freedom in this world to raise your voice of justice and to make your contribution in the help of the children of Kosova so that we can return in our birthplace, which is warm and to live in peace and freedom with respect."

> "Suffering and Misery in Kosova
> By A. M. Gashi
> Qatrom Camp, B7, #2
> 20 May 1999"

"Hello, and may this letter find you, my loving friends, well. I am called A. Gashi and I am a student in the 8th grade. I come from the small village of Suhareka. For centuries in a row, Kosova has been a place that has been put in slavery by the wild, uncontrolled, barbaric beasts. The worst war began in March 1998 in Drenic and afterwards all was included when there were massacres of old men, women and innocent children. The war also includes my loving birthplace, which I love so much, and for which I am even able to give my life, Suhareka. Suhareka was completely blockaded by the Serb police and soldiers. No one was allowed to go out into the street. The school, which had previously echoed with the sounds and noises of students, now is alone and in silence. People waited in their houses as though they were imprisoned. This was the first day of the week, Monday. All of a sudden, we heard sounds of automatic firing and pistols. We didn't know what had taken place. But afterwards we understood that one Serb policeman had been killed. After that took place, the Serb police blockaded every neighborhood of the little city, killing and treating badly the Albania families. After the murder took place, the Serbs were very upset and they killed seven Albanian men that were close with the relatives, which were women and children. The word came that we should forsake our homes. We did not know where to hide ourselves, where to go. We didn't know if they were going to kill us or if we would even be alive. We went out in undetermined directions, and we stopped in a village and even there they began to throw grenades. We left there, going from one village to another, but since the grenades kept on coming, we didn't rest. We went all night long without any rest or sleep in the snow. It was very cold and the wind was blowing. Even though we didn't rest and we were obligated to go on the village of Bellanica. As soon as we arrived in a grassy area, where others had arrived, the Serbs came and surrounded the village. Some of the police began to set fire to houses, whereas others were treating the people with violence in order to give them money. Even to the tractor where we were, the policeman came howling like a wolf and he was asking for money. He put bullets in his pocket, saying either give us money or they are going to execute the others. When we heard these words, we were frightened. Some of the police had black masks. In their hands, they had bottles of alcohol. One policeman, who had in his hand two bottles of beer, took from his pocket some of the signs of the KLA and said the Army for Freedom was the one that made us leave Kosova. Go to Albania, that is where you have your place. Leave this place because Kosova belongs to Serbia.

You are trespassers in this area. I wish that neither had come to help us in this moment that was so difficult. After many sufferings we went on to Albania. The mothers kept crying because they had left their sons in the war, in the lines of the KLA. The most difficult moment was when my father and three of my uncles returned to Kosova, as they were soldiers in the KLA. We traveled without bread and without water until we arrived in Albania. Now we are here in Qatrom in Korçë. I look at the sky at night with the stars and curse life and the Serbian regime that made us leave Kosova, our Kosova, our loving Kosova. Why are we not like other children of the world? I call you in the other places of Europe to do more for Kosova and the Kosovar children. We love Kosova. We want Kosova to be free and independent. We don't want toys."

"Our Sufferings During the War in Kosova
Albana M. G.
Qatrom Camp, Korçë, Albania
20 May 99"

"I greet you, loving friends. I am a student in the 8th grade. Let's leave aside 1998. I am going to tell you a tragedy that we have experienced in the year 1999. It has already occurred for a certain time that my little village had been filled with sadness. One day when we were surrounding our table, we heard that a Serb had been killed and from that day began all of the time of trouble, the biggest trouble of all of these years. We were alone. My dad for approximately one year had been in the forces of the KLA with his brothers. There were bullets dancing around in every corner of the house. The streets were filled with police and they were killing and beating many of the passersby at that moment. Word came that we needed, without exception, to leave our homes, so we went from one village to another, riding on the roads with our tractors. The Serbs kept on throwing those grenades without resting night and day.

We were obligated at night to wake up from our sleep to get up and go into a ditch where there was water. As often as we were thinking of sleeping because we were in restful sleep, around 2, 3 or 5 in the morning, we would have to move. We were in the mountains. It was very cold. On top of the tractor, we had nylon to put on. Many times, the rain fell with winds. We didn't have extra clothes because we didn't have time to get them when we went out of the house. We survived all of these things, but only to a certain point—the grenades and rockets we could not tolerate. All of the villages around us were attacked by grenades. We also left this village and we went to one that was further away from that one. And what do you think happened there? When it was the middle of the day, the Serbs began to cast grenades in that place. Later on, the whole village was surrounded by those merciless snakes, who from one side without had set fire to the houses and from the other side they killed and they beat the young people and the elderly people. They were seeking a lot of money. They didn't save their bullets, even from the children and their animals. They would come up running towards the tractor and they were pointing their automatic at us and calling out "money, money, otherwise we will kill you, everybody and we will take off your heads, so pull out your money quickly". They didn't come, just one or two, but everyone according to his own pleasure. They were saying you have loved A. Humashi and he is the one who has done this to you, leave now, go to him. You have sought and you have these consequences. What did you desire of the KLA? They are terrorists. They kill you and one man pulled out some signs of the KLA. They were saying that these were not going to exist ever again.

There was a terrible moment when they asked if we had any of our family as soldiers in the KLA, but they didn't wait for an answer. They kept speaking an Albanian word and another in their language. They said: "Turn your head away from Kosova and from this happiness because you are never going to return. Go to your brothers. They say they have you as brothers and they are going to leave you to die for a little bit of bread." In the end, they said "goodbye" in Albanian. We will meet you in Tirana. So, we set out towards Albania—two days without bread and without water and with sleep in our eyes. After a lot of suffering, we arrived in Albania. Now we are situated in Qatrom Camp. Here the conditions are very difficult, but the most difficult is the homesickness we have for our father, our uncles and for all of Kosova for which we suffer so much. We have a desire to return as quickly as possible to Kosova.

Why should we not be like other children in the entire world? Or are we different from them or have done something so terrible so that the Lord would curse us for all of our lives? I think this is not true life. I ask you to do even more to help us return as quickly as possible to Kosova and our relatives and become children of the world. World, how do you stand the war in Kosova? We are in the 20th century, and the war does not have a shadow. Instead of being able to live now in freedom in Kosova and to eat bread, we have only tears and bitterness. I repeat this one more time, I plead with you, do even more for us. We only love Kosova, free Kosova, and nothing else."

The concert ended. First, silence, then the audience erupted with clapping and cheering, proud of the children's ability to share their pain while creating a spirit of unity between the audience and the participants. The children glowed as they exited the stage and returned to their parents.

I needed time to absorb what I had witnessed. There were no words.

A Day Off

Sunday and a day off—the first since I arrived on 6 May. Relief from the stress and strain of working non-stop in the camp came none too soon. After breakfast at a local café and a cappuccino, Spiro, my driver, drove Genti and me to Drenovë, a small, rural village near Korçë. In contrast to the constant demands of the refugees, I stepped into a different world, a world of tranquil, rural living. Shepherds tended their sheep, while men in faded overalls tilled the land with their pitchforks, rakes and hoes. Tiny houses dotted the landscape. It was a step back in time, away from the hustle-bustle of modern life. Serenity washed over me like a welcomed spring rain, carrying away the tension and anxiety held in my body. The sweet smell of freshly tilled earth filled my senses; a gentle breeze swept across my face as the sun shone on my shoulders. My mind and body soaked in the ambiance of this peaceful village.

In the distance, I saw donkeys burdened with heavy bags of hay strapped to their backs. Their masters dragged them forward. The curiosity of a foreign visitor drew a crowd. Genti translated for the villagers and me. The women gathered around me while the men stood at a distance, leaning on their hoes and pitchforks. Although timid, the villagers greeted me with warmth and interest—the women inched closer and closer; the men touched their hats and nodded acknowledgment. I watched with fascination and awe as the women hand-spun shorn wool onto a spindle and then knitted directly onto the needles. The motion seemed continuous, natural and effortless. It was completely hypnotic. As a knitter, I could not imagine having to knit with this process—following a pattern with yarn in a ball challenged me. I marveled at the intricacy of design and colors.

"Is it possible for me to purchase something?" I asked.

Beaming with pride, they said, *"Po."* Running to their homes, they brought their finished projects to show.

I purchased a long runner for my entry hallway. The intricate, repeated design, in vibrant red, blue, green, yellow, and purple, was breathtaking. I also purchased a small area rug of blue and red. The tightly woven threads meant the rugs were reversible. Unable to observe the process, I pondered how they created such exquisite rugs. Thrilled with my purchases, I asked, "Would it be possible to bring your finished items to our house, where other international workers might purchase them?"

Giggles of excitement rippled between the women as they said, *"Po.* When could we come?"

We set a date and time, and it was time to leave. I longed to linger in this peaceful setting, observing the simplicity of their lives and seeing the beauty and pride in their faces and interacting with them. I was grateful for Genti, who enabled the conversation to flow. I spoke a few words in Albanian and in return, they smiled, emanating warmth and hospitality. The language of the heart flowed between us. Being the first American to visit their village, I saw they were as fascinated with me as I was with them.

Glowing with gratitude and peace, I returned to camp, renewed, and reinvigorated. The sounds of sheep bleating, the smells of freshly mowed hay, and the genuine warmth of the village people lingered in my memory.

Facts, Facts, Facts

UNHCR Kosovo Crisis Update: 25 May 1999[1]
AT A GLANCE

Around 10,000 Kosovars flee into Albania and the FYR of Macedonia on 24 May. The figure includes nearly 1,500 refugees who went to Albania and more than 8,500 to the FYR of Macedonia. Despite continuing tensions in the border region, several hundred Kosovars manage to cross into Montenegro from Kosovo. Departures under the humanitarian evacuation program on Monday total 1,142 bringing the overall count to date more than 62,000. An estimated 772,000 refugees and displaced people are in the region, including 64,200 in Montenegro, 246,700 in the FYR of Macedonia, 439,500 in Albania and 21,500 in Bosnia and Herzegovina.

Major Developments
ALBANIA

On Monday, more than 1,400 refugees arrived at the Morini

---

[1] UN High Commissioner for Refugees (UNHCR), 25 May 1999

border crossing, including a further 216 released prisoners from Smrekrovnica prison in Kosovska Mitrovica in northern Kosovo. As the refugees were coming in, two shots were fired across the border, the bullets coming close to UNHCR staff on duty. Monday's arrival brought to 6,000 the number of Kosovars who had entered Albania over the past four days. Meanwhile, the organized relocation of refugees from temporary camps in Kukes to southern Albania using NATO vehicles started Tuesday morning.

Eighty-five refugees — part of the 200 planned to be moved during the day — were transported in the morning on 10 NATO to Camp Hope, a few kilometers from Fier in southern Albania. The trip takes seven to nine hours. Camp Hope, built by the American military, will eventually have a capacity of some 20,000 refugees. It currently holds 3,000 refugees. On Sunday, about 1,900 refugees were transported on 40 buses and seven trucks and tractor-wagons to the south from Kukes.

As the influx into Albania goes on, construction of tented camps and communal shelters continue. There are 49 tented camps in 12 prefectures in Albania, including 16 which have been completed, and 33 which are still under construction. In addition, 287 communal centers have been registered, of which 128 are now occupied and the rest are in various stages of completion. Of the 440,000 refugees in Albania, more than 81,000 are in tented camps and around 73,000 are in communal centers — sports centers, schools and public buildings. The rest of refugees — more than a quarter of a million people are staying with host families.

As facilities operated on a bilateral basis are being handed over to UNHCR, its staff are attempting to provide a sustainable standard of assistance in all the camps and refugee centers. Over the past week, UNHCR has signed six agreements worth $3 million to accelerate response to emergency needs. So far, 31 projects are in place, covering distribution of basic and complementary food and such items as blankets, mattresses, sleeping bags, jerry cans and plastic sheets. Other projects include improvement of water, sanitation and health services. UNHCR has started the first distribution of new standard food basket in the camps and collective centers. New agreements with bakeries have been signed for bread production. The Red Cross is gradually taking over assistance to host families, including "cash for shelter program" by the Swiss government initially for 6,500 families. Planning for winterization continues. A team of Albanian engineers has assessed potential collective buildings what could house 20,000 refugees during winter.

FYR of Macedonia

Two trains and 13 buses offloaded more than 8,500 refugees at the FYR of Macedonia border on Monday. After some delays, police agreed to move refugees from the border and the Blace holding area into camps. The majority of arrivals were transported to the Stenkovec and Cegrane camps and the rest remained at the holding area. Registration of the arrival went very quickly, witnessed during the evening by visiting British and American delegations and the FYR of Macedonia Minister of Interior, along with UNHCR staff. The refugees came mostly from Pristina, Urosevac and Vitina. They said Serbian forces were conduction a systematic "ethnic cleansing" operation in these areas. Many said they originally came from Podujevo, the strategic town along the Pristina-Belgrade Road, and they claimed massacres have taken place in the villages. Yugoslav troops have been conducting an offensive again the Kosovo Liberation Army in the Podujevo region since December of last year. Thousand more refugees were reported to be heading toward the frontier from the interior of Kosovo. UNHCR staff and government officials braced for another massive wave of arrivals on Tuesday.

Secret Service Police, the Bread Saga, and Other Interruptions

Although I had only been in camp for three weeks, it felt like six months. Time blurred, adrenaline constantly flowed, work never ended, the internet crashed, translators went missing when I needed them most. Each day brought distractions, often chaotic demands that required immediate attention.

I granted permission for one of the Albanian staff to have three nights off in Tirana. Then I took my computer to Qatrom to work on the list of community leaders (names, clusters, and tent numbers). Next, we distributed Pampers. During the distribution, a community leader told me that two tents had burned down the previous evening. Everything halted. An immediate investigation yielded empty tents burned to the ground, but no injuries. As the examination concluded, a Secret Service police officer arrived with no identification, stating he needed to find a refugee, an alleged spy. Per RI rules, we did not allow unidentified persons into the camp. As I escorted him to the gate, I said, "You need to wait outside the camp perimeter until I can verify your credentials, since I am not authorized to allow unidentified persons into Qatrom. I am sure you can understand. Please give me your contact information, and I will get back to you." I did not know how to tell if someone was legitimate or not.

I asked Jeff F to talk to the secret service police while I went to the NATO KFOR area to ask for help. The KFOR major verified the legitimacy of the officer; therefore, he had free access to walk around the camp in secret. Although we did not have the name of the alleged refugee spy, I didn't particularly appreciate that the officer could roam around freely. I knew this would unsettle the refugee population—another unanswered situation. I never learned if there was a spy among the refugees or if the secret service police located anyone.

During the camp self-management (CSM) board, I explained the situation that the secret service police were looking for an alleged spy. Then we discussed the need to fulfill a request to reunite an eight-year-old girl in Macedonia with her parents in Qatrom. I never learned how the girl separated from her family. How frightening that must have been for the family. I could not imagine the fear of my grandchildren being separated from my son and my daughter-in-law. Official inspectors interrupted our meeting to inspect our bread. One half of the delivered bread was filled with insects. We agreed to meet with the World Food Program (WFP), CARE, and the food committee leaders to visit the UNHCR-designated local bakery that provided the bread at 3 PM. When we toured the facility, we found filth everywhere. No standardized protocols had been implemented. The inspectors agreed to work with WFP, CARE, and the Salvation Army to find a solution.

The day continued when the European Union (EU) watch group popped in to ensure everything was okay. They came every other day or so for an update on the KLA activity. As they left, UNHCR arrived to introduce me to a legal officer from Tirana who wanted to discuss security. Another issue demanded my attention, and I forgot about him. By the time I remembered, he had left. My embarrassment didn't last long, as two women from Dorkas arrived to help sort clothes. I started them working with our teen volunteer staff while I grabbed time to work on the committee list, which I had started in the morning. I arrived home at 8 PM, exhausted and hungry.

Questions from a Friend

With no TV available and all the newsprint written in Albanian, we relied on the UNHCR briefings for updates centered on the refugee concerns. We received little information about the war in Kosovo. It made for interesting conversations with friends back home. Even though I was "on the ground", the scope of what I knew was somewhat limited. When refugees arrived in camp, they said that the Serbian forces continued to evacuate villages throughout Kosovo.

My friend Edie asked, "Do you think the hostility will be resolved before winter?"

"Everything is up in the air—rumors of an agreement float around daily. If an agreement isn't signed, plans for winterizing thirty government buildings in Korçë are under review. Several NGOs working in the area and the prefekture (local government) will determine the buildings. It gets cold in mid-September, so contingency plans are needed."

"What are the rumors there?"

"You probably hear more than we do, since there is no television and no English newspapers. With little time to browse the internet most of us compete for the one access line to write home. UNHCR said that 150,000 refugees are on the move, leaving Kosovo and heading toward the Macedonia border. The area creates a bottleneck in a place they call 'no-man's-land,' which is between the borders of Kosovo and Macedonia. We are on a 24-hour alert to receive refugees with a projection of 400 per day arriving over the next ten days. Housing the refugees in this area is problematic since the additional camps have not been completed, adding stress to an already stressful situation."

"Is Milošević backing down?"

"I have no idea, but I doubt it. Kosovo is still a part of Serbia. Yesterday, I worked from 8 AM to midnight—today, I am exhausted—hard to think about that."

"What will the refugees find when they return?"

"Landmines are a problem. I know KFOR (Kosovo Force, part of NATO) will proceed when an agreement is signed to rid the return routes of landmines. One of the refugees who arrived the other day said roads, bridges, and utilities had been destroyed as well as businesses and homes. Kosovo will look like a war zone with destruction everywhere. I know the refugees here are desperate to return home, and it will take dedication and determination to rebuild that destroyed land. Also, a new government will need to be established. Right now, I can only concentrate on the refugees in Qatrom, and it isn't easy to think beyond the day-to-day concerns here. I would go crazy if I had to think about all the politics. Please keep asking questions. It gives me a spark to hear from everyone. I so appreciate our friendship."

Asking for the Impossible

> *"How wonderful it is that nobody need wait a single moment before starting to improve the world."*
>
> *- Anne Frank*

Joy rippled through Qatrom with the birth of a baby, although it was difficult for the mother, who required a Caesarean section after a long labor. We learned of the birth upon arriving after our UNHCR morning briefing. At 9:30 AM, the ten-year-old daughter arrived at the RI compound to request baby clothes, Pampers, bottles, and a baby bed for the newborn. Two of our refugee volunteers, Drita and Yeta, volunteered to look for baby clothes.

Drita, tall with long, curly, black hair and sparkling brown eyes, bonded immediately with Yeta, who was petite with short, inky-colored hair, small facial features, and a winning smile. Although they came from different villages in Kosovo, they were inseparable. Being the only female volunteers, they brought joy and gentleness to the teenage volunteer team. They worked well with the boys, withstood their banter, and returned it with ease and sparkle. It boosted my energy to be with them. I marveled at the teamwork and ethics of the teen volunteers.

After lunch, the daughter reappeared with another request. "My mother has difficulty nursing. She needs a burner to sterilize the water for the formula."

I replied, "We don't have burners."

"Will RI tap into the local power source of Korçë and run a power line to our tent?" she asked.

I blinked and replied, "No, it is illegal to tap into the governmental electrical grid. I will ask if the Salvation Army can heat water for your mother."

She scowled, turned in a huff, and stomped away.

My brain whirred. How did other mothers sterilize the water? How many mothers nursed their babies? The water from the taps was good, but not sterile for baby formula. Could the Salvation Army sterilize water and store it in jerry cans for the mothers? I asked Marci and Joanne to brainstorm with me. Marci said, "I have a good rapport with the MDM staff and could ask them if they would sterilize the water for formula." MDM agreed to help.

Drita and Yeta said they would locate the young girl and her mother to tell them about our solution. Upon their return, they said that the mother was unsatisfied and demanded MDM sterilize the water every three hours.

At times like this, we wanted to throw our hands up in despair because some situations got to be too much. We decided we had done all we could, and it was up to the mother to resolve her differences with MDM. Since we heard nothing further, we assumed they reached a solution.

Some Days Are More Difficult than Others

"It is your reaction to adversity, not the adversity itself, that determines how your life's story will develop."
                                                            - Dieter F. Uchtdorf

Sustaining workdays from 8 AM to midnight created fatigue. Fatigue clouded my thinking, deprived me of sound judgment, dampened my sense of humor, and lessened my tolerance to meet daily challenges. Yesterday, Xhevat continued his constant demands and negativity. Instead of quelling the refugees' agitation during the near riot over bread filled with insects, he exacerbated the situation by encouraging the refugees to harass the Salvation Army workers who served the bread. When I asked Xhevat to control the crowd, he glared defiantly and said, *"Jo!"* Then he turned his back on me.

Later, during the camp self-management, Xhevat dominated the conversation by disallowing the other members to speak. Through my interpreter, I said, *"Mirembrema* [Good afternoon], we need volunteers to monitor the gate at the entrance to avoid unwelcome individuals from entering Qatrom. Can you come up with solutions?" Qatrom, unlike most refugee camps, had freedom of movement for the refugees to enter and return at will.

Xhevat stood, leaned forward and planted his hands on the table, saying, "No one can volunteer unless RI pays them."

My eyes drilled into his, "Xhevat, *jo*, you know the policy of UNHCR does not pay the volunteers."

Feeling emboldened, Xhevat grabbed my arm and said, "Ah, all the NGOs working in Qatrom have to report to me instead of RI management."

"Xhevat, let go of my arm."

He let go of my arm but continued, "There needs to be a contractual agreement between the Albanian and Kosovo governments in Tirana regarding schooling for the Kosovar children in Qatrom."

Stepping away in a calm, firm voice, I said, "We have no authority to make requests to the government."

Xhevat tried to stonewall me at every turn. Although feelings of frustration and turmoil surged inside me, I kept my mouth shut. Instead, I stiffened my body and plastered a smile on my face while I listened to him rant — all throughout using interpreters.

After five minutes, I said, "I acknowledge your concerns." Turning on my heel, I walked away with my interpreter. I was seething. I willed myself to remain poised and keep my thoughts to myself — time for a team meeting. I remembered the words of Zig Ziglar, "Sometimes, adversity is what you need to face, in order to become successful." Sometimes, it can be more difficult than at other times. That day was one of those times for me.

Morava Mountains

The siren call of the craggy Morava Mountains nagged at me day after day. Their rugged strength and constancy reminded me to remain strong. The lure of them heightened after Marci and Joanna hiked to the top, where Marci took a gorgeous aerial view of Qatrom and the surrounding farming fields. I wanted to see it for myself. Time to act. One afternoon off, I said, "Elton, would you like to hike up the mountain with me?"

"Of course," he said.

I donned my hiking boots and grabbed my water bottle, sunscreen, hat, and a snack. Spiro dropped us off at the trailhead, a narrow dirt road covered in loose rocks, some the size of small boulders. The afternoon sun was bright and warm, and a gentle breeze helped cool us as we hiked, although the loose rocks slowed my progress. After climbing for half an hour, we came to a bend in the road where we saw a man yanking at the reins of a donkey burdened with uneven stacks of wood. Expletives exploded from his lips as he tugged, whip in hand. Yet, the donkey refused to move. I gasped in horror. Just as I was saying, "Elton, that load is too heavy for the donkey," the wood tumbled from the donkey and scattered over the narrow road, making it impossible to pass.

Looking at me, Elton said, "I will help the man reload the wood onto the donkey. I'll make sure the wood is more secure and distributed better."

My enthusiasm for hiking fizzled—I cannot tolerate cruelty to animals. When Elton finished, I said, "Let's go back." The sight of the donkey lingered in my mind as we returned. I called Spiro on my radio and asked him to meet us. I never found another chance to hike into the mountains, but the desire never left me.

One Sunday morning in late May, Spiro offered to drive me to the top of the near 7,000-foot Morava Mountains where a giant white cross stood like a beacon for the valley below. One of the Korçë police officers greeted us. Although he did not speak English, he pointed to the Church of St. Elias, which offered a respite for weary travelers. Picnic tables and seating areas speckled the well-manicured landscape around the church parking lot. Several lookout spots provided excellent panoramic views of Korçë and the valley. Qatrom looked orderly and pristine, devoid of chaos and trauma. Distance gave me a different perspective, a clearer view of what was important. With no translator present, Spiro and I spoke little. The serenity of the moment was the only language needed. After admiring the vistas, the police officer departed, and we returned. I said, "*Efharisto*, Spiro, *efharisto*." (Thank you in Greek—the only Greek word I know.) Spiro nodded as a grin spread across his face. Once again, I remembered a word in another language could mean so much to another person—another simple pleasure.

Sensitive Topics

A busload of 100 new refugees queued outside the white community tent to register and to receive a tent assignment, bedding, etc., on a blistering hot day. During the registration, Ron C., who worked for the U.S. Department of State, entered the tent and pulled me outside. He needed to collect evidence of war crimes. Members of his team showed up unannounced at all times during the day.

With a serious expression on his face, Ron said, "First, I wanted you to know Milošević has been charged with war crimes. Second, the reason more refugees are not coming here is that they prefer to stay in Macedonia, as Albania doesn't allow resettlement to another country."

"Oh, no wonder we aren't getting the expected numbers of refugees. Delighted to hear about Milošević." I said, "On another issue, several single men are arriving here, adding to the increased possibility of rape. As a precaution, we set up a security committee to patrol at night, but the women tell the medical staff they trust very few men. Last night, the RI men circulated the camp until 1 AM. Could you pass along our concerns?"

"Yes, I'll let the State Department know."

"Thanks, I appreciate that. I wanted you to know. It would also be helpful if we had advanced notice when your team will be here."

By the time Ron and I finished talking, the registration and distribution concluded. Time to meet with the refugee board.

"*Mirembrema*," I said as I entered the meeting tent. Everyone was gathered around the table. I drew in a deep breath and through my interpreter, I said, "We are very fortunate we have had no deaths in Qatrom. However, I want us to be prepared. Please, could you tell me your traditions and procedures regarding the burial of a loved one? What preparations are needed?"

They murmured between themselves. After looking around the table, a tall man stood, saying that "the body is washed, then wrapped in a white sheet that must come from a mosque. The body is placed on a slant board [the translation was difficult on this point], while the family stays with the body for twenty-four hours before burial. Where can someone be buried?"

"*Faleminderit*," I said. "To answer your question, the prefekt has given land for burial. I will see if I can get the white cloth. However, you need to understand that legally, the police and the health department require notification to issue a death certificate."

The committee nodded to me and to one another. I knew they understood I wanted to honor their traditions. As they left, each member embraced me and said, "*Faleminderit*." After they left, teary-eyed, I turned to Xhilda and said, "Thank you, you did a wonderful job translating."

Tears rolled down her cheeks as she said, "Thank you for caring."

Days later, the cloth from a mosque arrived. I never learned where Jeff found it. I was just grateful he was able to locate it. Although we never had to use it, we were prepared.

Children's Football Tournament

"Laughter is the sun that drives winter from the human face."
- Victor Hugo

The sun burst over the mountains. A buzz of excitement cascaded through Qatrom. Preparations for the football tournament were under way. Sabri selected teams by age. With no uniforms available, teams divided into shirts versus no shirts. Goals were set in place, the playing field marked, and referees assigned. The games would begin after school and lunch.

Before the tournament, fourteen journalists from around the world arrived that morning. With so many, Marci and I agreed to interview together. Vying for attention, each journalist shouted out questions:

"When will the new refugees arrive from Macedonia?"
"How many refugees are in Qatrom?"
"How do the refugees occupy their time?"
"What restrictions are there?"
"When will the conflict end?"

It was a barrage of inquiries. Marci and I decided rather than trying to answer while the journalists shouted over each other, we would take them on a walk through Qatrom. We would answer their questions along the way, and they could see for themselves what life was like in the camp. After the tour, with their questions answered, the journalists seemed impressed with the camp's organization and activities for the children. Many wanted to stay for the tournament but had to leave to file their reports.

Genti approached me and said, "I have a friend who works for the BBC; she would like to interview you."

I said, "Yes, have her come at 1:30 PM before the football tournament."

After the interview, she said, "I understand why Genti works here instead of being a journalist."

"Thank you, and it is an honor and a privilege to work here. I will pass along your compliment to everyone. Now it is time to watch the football tournament. Would you like to attend?"

We walked together to the field. The crowd had gathered to cheer their teams to victory. We arrived in time to see the captains go to the center for the coin toss to decide which team would kick off first.

Whooping and hollering erupted as someone scored a goal, followed by a cacophony of applause. The coaches ran up and down the field, yelling words of encouragement and instructions. The air was electric.

Dragging myself away from the game, I embarked on a quest to locate prizes. Drita and Yeta helped, and together we found awards from a box of trinkets. In the distance, we heard cheers and pots and pans banging as the game progressed.

By late afternoon, the tournament ended. The winning team was ecstatic. They received their trophies, and the Salvation Army served cookies and lemonade for everyone. Sweaty and tired, everyone enjoyed the afternoon of games and camaraderie. An ambiance of light-heartedness swept through Qatrom as the refugees lingered before returning to their tents.

Bucket Brigade

"Necessity is the mother of invention."
- Attributed to Plato's Republic

After the incident when the two unoccupied tents burned down, I realized we had not discussed what to do in case of a fire. We were grateful no one was injured, but we could not risk another fire without a plan in place. Questions regarding the cause of the fire would have to wait until we determined proper fire procedures, which slipped through the cracks as activities swirled, and competing issues arose during the first six weeks of opening Qatrom.

Finally, I found the time to gather the teenage volunteers together and tell them, "We need to have a mock fire drill training. Find as many buckets as possible and meet at the water tap in Section C10."

Turning to my interpreters, I said, "Please go to each cluster and locate any firefighters from Kosovo to assist us." Next, I radioed Marci, "Please order fire extinguishers, hoses, and buckets for sand and water. We need them in the camp. Also, we are about to begin a mock fire drill if you would like to participate. Thanks."

Within a half-hour, the volunteers gathered at the designated water tap.

"The line will start at the water tap to fill the buckets. Pass the filled buckets along the line to tent number ten," I instructed the group.

Water sloshed and spilled, soaking us as the buckets moved down the line. It was awkward at first, but giggles soon turned to concentration. We found our rhythm as everyone grappled with the seriousness of the situation. Meanwhile, my interpreters returned with an experienced firefighter from Kosovo.

"Will you be willing to organize and train each section on fire prevention and bucket brigade?" I asked. "Also, will you determine the best fire lane for each section along with escape routes?"

"Yes, I live in Section A1. Let's start there."

We gathered the buckets and proceeded to A1. The refugee firefighter directed the bucket brigade to douse an empty tent with water for practice.

A refugee stormed from his tent with clenched fists and arms flailing over his head, bellowing in Albanian, "What are you doing?"

The firefighter apologized, saying in Albanian, "We thought the tent was empty. Please forgive us. We are performing a mock fire drill because two tents caught on fire. Luckily, no one was hurt. We will conduct mock fire drills in each section of Qatrom, so everyone will know what to do if there is another fire."

I saw the other man's body relax, and his tone softened. Then he gathered a bucket and joined in. I heard him say something. Everyone laughed and agreed. My interpreter told me he said, "Let's just practice without throwing water on anyone's tent."

With the crisis averted and fire drill procedures established, we breathed a sigh of relief. The next day, the Kosovar firefighter began to implement trainings section by section. I tried to learn how the fire started, but the refugees remained silent, although rumors surfaced about teens meeting in vacant tents at night with candles.

Although candles were forbidden, many mothers told the

medical staff they burned candles at night because their children, still traumatized, were frightened of the dark. They also used small propane burners to boil water for coffee and tea. One night when I was on patrol, I saw lights in a handful of tents. Puzzled, I learned the refugee electricians siphoned electricity from the town's pole lights. With the archaic power plant, electrical dips and power outages occurred frequently. I wondered if the siphoned electricity added to the problem.

Children's drawings at the exhibition

Qatrom Art Exhibition

A flurry of activity rippled through Qatrom. The children made artwork with donated watercolor paint, crayons, pencils and paper. The medical staff encouraged the children to draw pictures as a means of therapy to mitigate the trauma of war. At the end of May, teachers and students converted the enormous community tent into an art gallery with the drawings displayed on the walls. Children and teachers darted in and out of the tent with supplies and artwork. RI invited UNHCR, the British KFOR, and other NGOs in the area to attend the 2 PM opening.

The tent flap doors opened, and we inched along from drawing to drawing, shocked by the horror and darkness the children had witnessed. The images of guns, tanks, bullets, blood, burning homes, and caravans of people fleeing from war and devastation flew from the paper into our hearts. There was mostly silence, broken by an occasional gasp or quiet weeping. A quiet so deep, it sounded thunderous. The impact of the images jolted my senses. Tears streamed down my cheeks as I looked at each child standing by his or her drawing, and I saw the lingering pain and fear in their eyes. No child should experience what they had witnessed.

As I turned a corner to enter another section, I stopped. My eyes fell on a drawing of a vase of colorful flowers resting on a table. Pausing, I drank in the beauty of the flowers and saw the promise of life and hope, which shined like a beam of light amidst the darkness. Beside her drawing, a twelve-year-old girl stood with a radiant smile. I pulled her close to me in a hug and thanked her, marveling at how a child of twelve could see hope and beauty amongst the destruction.

The horror of what these children had witnessed sank into our hearts. I wondered if they would ever heal or would the trauma lodge deep within them forever? Would PTSD return again and again, triggered by an unsuspecting noise or smell? We left the tent that day, but the images and my heartache for the children have never left me.

Explosion

Marci, Joanne, and I sat enjoying a warm, delicious meal of lamb stew, tomato and cucumber salad, and peach slices for dessert, when an explosion lifted us from our seats.

"Damn, that was close!" Marcie yelled. "I'm so tired of these explosions!" We knocked over our chairs as we rushed to the second-floor balcony to see how close the explosion had come to our house.

The police dashed from all directions towards the scene of the explosion before disappearing from our sight. We couldn't see anything else. We grumbled that this was the third time in the past week that grenade explosions and gunfire erupted and how unsettling they were. A couple of weeks earlier, a grenade exploded close to where we held our UNHCR briefings. We could see the crater where the grenade landed. That explosion killed one person and wounded two others.

Someone pounding on the front door caught our attention. We left the balcony and cautiously went to the front door.

"Who is it?" Marci asked.

Through the closed door, a voice said, "We are the police to tell you to stay inside. These attacks were not directed toward the relief workers." Relief workers were often targets of violence. "They are grudge or gang related incidents. Don't walk at night. You might be caught in the crossfire." Although shaken, we thanked the officers.

These words were not comforting to us, but they served as another clear warning to be diligent. Our hearts still pounding with the flow of adrenaline, we made our way back to the dinner table to finish our now cold meal and our conversation on the perpetual problem of stealing. We made a pact to protect each other and to never to walk alone.

Tragedy Strikes

I woke thinking of my grandson, Kristopher, who would have been celebrating his eleventh birthday. Kristopher died of a cerebral hemorrhage from a freak fall in 1993. To ease the emptiness and pain in my heart, I grabbed my pen and paper and wrote. Words flowed as I recalled our times together, treasuring and savoring each precious moment. As I wrote, a warm glow of love filled my heart, lessening the pain of loss—I felt grateful for the five and a half years we had together. My healing continued bit by bit. Then work called.

Being Sunday, we had a skeleton crew at Qatrom. Jeff, RI headquarters, Elton, and I arrived around 9 AM. A refugee greeted us and beckoned us to follow him to one of our cluster leaders' tent. At the entrance was a chair draped with a white towel and a photograph of two young men pinned to it. I asked Elton why it was there.

Elton explained, "The chair with a towel signifies death, so everyone will come to pay their respects to the bereaved family."

Not knowing who had died, we entered the tent. The family huddled together on the mattress, as there were no chairs inside. The father, a slender man, stood and greeted us, his face shaded by grief. The man told us through Elton "My eighteen-year-old son joined the KLA three months ago and was killed in action. My wife's brother was with him, so she lost her son and her seventeen-year-old brother."

Filled with fresh memories of my grief, I embraced him. His wife was sobbing and clutching a three-month-old baby. She looked at me with pleading eyes. I lowered myself to the mattress and wrapped my arms around her and the baby. She wept into my shoulder as I held them both. We cried as her grief mingled with mine. She handed me the baby while she searched for a photo of her son. The picture showed her son and brother looking proud in their KLA uniforms. Elton interpreted as she said, "This was taken three weeks before they were killed."

The father said, "I cannot cry as my son died defending our country."

Then they introduced me to the other children, a girl, fourteen, and a boy, ten—both bewildered, huddled together on another mattress. The mother murmured something to her daughter, who stood and offered us tea and a piece of candy. Tradition dictated serving food and drink as people paid their respects. I rocked the baby in my arms, whispering soft sounds of comfort while holding the mother's hand. They talked of Kosovo, their family, and their life.

The father said, "I was a TV/electronics professional until the Serbs refused to let me work. Then I became a carpenter until they forced us from our home."

As others came to pay their respect, we prepared to leave. Placing my hands over my heart, I turned to the mother and said, *"Me vjen keq.* [I am sorry]. I understand. I lost my grandson. His birthday is today."

We embraced again, feeling each other's grief as only mothers can.

I needed time to myself. I took the rest of the day off. Later Xhilda and I walked around the town, stopping at a café for a coffee. It felt good to breathe in the sense of everyday living. I took photos as we strode through shaded streets and neighborhoods, watching families as they passed. I took a seat on a wooden bench to enjoy a serene park. The time was priceless. It afforded me a much-needed escape, but also a chance to develop a more intimate relationship with Xhilda.

Goodbye Party for British KFOR

B reaking news hit in early June: The British KFOR received orders to pull up stakes and head to Kosovo for their intended mission. With the peace talks underway, the NATO forces in Kosovo had to remove land mines, oversee the orderly removal of the Yugoslav Military Forces and the Serbian Police, quell the KLA fighting, and establish peace keeping procedures.

RI staff received an invitation to attend the goodbye party at 1800 hours. Meanwhile, Qatrom buzzed with the everyday activities like distribution, interviews by the U.S. Department of State and new arrivals. In addition, Xhilda, Drita, and Yeta went from section to section, tent by tent, to document the number of children by age and sex. RI and UNHCR needed the information for planning purposes.

As the end of the day approached, we saw a flurry of activity at the KFOR compound. The party was in full swing by the time we arrived. Row after row of tables and chairs filled the compound tent. Paper plates, plastic flatware and paper napkins were stacked like soldiers at the beginning of the buffet food table. Trays of hot and cold dishes, ham and cheese platters, a variety of salads, and an assortment of fruit and breads tantalized our taste buds. A dessert table displayed delicious Greek pastries. The amber colored Korçë beer flowed from tapped kegs. Chatter and laugher flowed as the NGOs and KFOR personnel mingled. Lights flashed as partygoers snapped photos of friends and good times.

As dusk turned to evening, everyone piled out of the tent for a goodbye photo. Many of us lingered, wanting to savor the moments. By the end of the next day, all the equipment, tents, satellite, and barbed wire fences would be gone, leaving an empty field in the condition it was before their arrival—an open space beside Qatrom.

The goodbyes meant a loss. Loss of security at Qatrom—having the British KFOR adjacent to Qatrom, provided extra protection for the refugees. With their departure, the threat of assault from the local population and traffickers increased. Loss of the respite to unwind during the daily briefings after a long, arduous day. Loss of hearing English spoken. The loss of new friends, knowing I would never see them again. The loss tore at my heart, yet the grateful memory of the experiences remained.

The following day, the lonely field stood, void of the activity of the British KFOR. They had built the complex in one day and left without a trace in one day—only the memory and my gratitude to them remained.

Not on My Watch

With the British KFOR gone, security threats heightened. In the dead of night, a group of local men with knives snuck into the camp to rob the refugees. The refugee men chased them away. The same day, a small security committee of refugees formed to patrol throughout the day and night, keeping a vigilant eye for disturbances or trouble.

The next night, a group of teenage boys gathered to party in an empty tent. Music blared. The nearby refugees could not sleep and complained to their leaders. After repeated requests to lower the music failed, a couple of refugee patrolmen stormed into the tent, bashed the boom box, and smacked the boys around.

Mehani, the father of the most badly beaten teenager, became so enraged he threatened to harm Fatom, a former KLA soldier who had been on patrol. Other parents joined in the demand for Fathom's removal from the camp—too much violence had occurred. Violence could not be perpetuated or tolerated in Qatrom. During my meeting with the board that afternoon, they expelled the ex-KLA fighter. Several board members escorted him out. Even with Fatom gone, tensions remained high. Mehani continued to rant and disrupt the other refugees, causing rumors of trouble to circulate.

Cindy, the RI therapist, Genti, and I met with the Mehani family to listen to their concerns and find a workable solution. At the Mehani tent, I instructed my driver to reverse the vehicle and keep it running in case of trouble. I requested UNHCR send a representative, although no one showed. During our meeting, an eruption exploded outside. Fatom sauntered into Qatrom against orders not to return.

A crowd descended on him. Hearing the disturbance, we all rushed from the tent. Seeing Fatom, Mehani grabbed a huge rock and hurled it at him. Fatom's knees buckled, falling to the ground as the rock struck. Blood spurted from his head. The angry crowd moved in closer. They kicked Fatom in the face, ribs, back, and stomach as he lay in a fetal position trying to protect his head with his arms. Fueled by anger and frustration, Mehani smashed the rock in Fatom's face — each blow fiercer and more robust. Someone fired two shots from a gun. The crowd went silent, stood, and looked around in search of the origin of the sound. *Who had a gun? Was anyone shot?*

Cindy yanked me behind the vehicle. I could not tear my eyes from the horror of the scene. My heart raced and adrenaline surged through me. A sudden power of determination and courage filled me — Not on my watch!

After seeing a fleeing teenager chased by the man with the gun sprint toward the perimeter fence with the imminent gunfire danger averted, I shouted to the driver, "Drive slowly into the crowd. We need to get Fatom to safety and medical attention."

We jumped into the vehicle. It inched slowly, forcing the crowd to disperse. We reached Fatom. Blood poured from the deep gashes in his head, his handsome face swollen beyond recognition. His robust and muscular body bent over as agonizing groans escaped his lips. Genti, Cindy, and I grabbed him, helping him stand and get in the back seat of the vehicle. Angry voices and waving clenched fists of the crowd followed us as we left for the medical tent. Our eyes riveted on them as we drove away. Strong during the crisis, my body started to react. I felt the pent-up tension in my body begin to release. However, my legs would not stop trembling. As we approached the medical tent with Fatom, Francisco, our lawyer volunteer, arrived on the scene.

I asked him to contact UNHCR, the local police, and our team to meet at the compound. We need to make hard decisions.

With Fathom's wounds cleaned and bandaged, we brought him to the compound, waiting for everyone to gather. We discussed the best solution for the safety of all concerned. Fatom knew people in another town and signed an agreement he would not return to Qatrom. The local police promised to escort Fathom. As he left, he thanked me.

"You saved my life, and I am beholden to you," he said.

I have thought about this incident over the years. I knew a power greater than I watched over me that terrifying day.

Next on the agenda: What to do with the Mehani family?

Consequences followed incidences. Fearing reprisal, Mehani's teenage son, Besim, fled Qatrom. Dusk fell over the camp. Panic set in when Besim did not show for dinner. Where was he? Everyone scoured Qatrom, but Besim could not be found. Grabbing Genti and Francesco, the volunteer lawyer, we sped to camp to talk with Mehani, who was distraught with anguish. I brought him to the compound tent where we could talk in private.

I said, "I understand your fear and anxiety. I have two sons, and I can only imagine how you feel. Please take a few breaths and try to think where he might be. We will search until we find him."

Still flushed with anger and fear, his clenched fists began to relax, and his breathing became less shallow. He said, "We have relatives in the mountains."

Spiro knew the area. I asked one of the staff to stay with Mehani while Genti, Francesco and I drove into the mountains. We chased one lead after another to no avail until the early hours of the morning. Exhaustion set in — yet we continued.

Turning to me, Francesco said, "I think we should take you back to the house to sleep while we continue."

"I can't stop until we find him. I am a mother and I know how much the fear is affecting Mehani. Thank you, Francesco. I appreciate your thoughtfulness"

At 2:30 AM, with no more leads and heavy hearts, we went home. Although we felt drained, sleep eluded us. Tension and unrest permeated the camp. Shaken by the incident of gunfire and violence of the afternoon, Genti stood in the shower for an hour when he returned home.

Morning dawned—no signs of Besim. I knew I had to speak with Mehani. Holding back tears, I told him we would start a new search. We would find his son. Just as we turned onto the dirt road leading away from Qatrom, we saw Besim dragging himself toward camp. Besim got into the car, and we sped back to camp, spewing dirt and dust along the roadside. Genti spoke to him about the frantic anxiety he created with his family and the staff. Upon arrival, Genti delivered the teen to his father. *I'm glad I wasn't the teen for that reunion, as I knew the father had quite a temper.* Cheers erupted as father and son ran towards each other with open arms. Relief rippled through the camp—everyone in Qatrom could identify with the terror of a lost child.

Anger and hostility toward the family lingered. After careful consideration, I contacted CARE International to see if they could host the family, as removal seemed like the only solution.

After summoning Mehani to the compound, I said, "I told you I was the mother of two sons. I understand your frustration, fear and anxiety. I must consider the safety of you and your family and protecting all the refugees in Qatrom. What are your thoughts?"

He said, "I want my family safe."

I laid my hands over his shaking hands. "That is also my concern. For the safety of all, CARE International offered to take all of you. CARE will provide for all your needs, although you will be the only refugees in the camp right now."

Hesitating for a few minutes, Mehani said, "I will move my family. I promise none of us will return to Qatrom."

"Thank you for your understanding. We all have heard the rumors of an impending peace agreement and I promise to deliver in person any pertinent news of the war or any peace agreement."

We embraced in a bittersweet goodbye. Mehani collected his family and belongings, and then Pierre, the CARE camp manager, drove them to the other camp. Mehani and his family took a piece of my heart. I visited them every few days to see how they were doing.

Former President Sali Bersiha visits camp

Dignitaries Visit Qatrom

On June 5 at the daily meeting, UNHCR announced the former president of Albania, Sali Berisha (1992-1997), would be arriving for a visit to Qatrom in just a few hours. Not much time to prepare. By the time we arrived at the camp, word of the visit had circulated amongst the refugees. *How word traveled like wildfire within the camp population continued to mystify me.* Genti and I quickly inspected the RI compound and each section to ensure tidiness.

A loud roar broke the usual hum of voices. We knew Mr. Berisha had arrived. Genti grabbed my camera as a throng of refugees swept us along. Three bodyguards angled around Mr. Berisha to keep the crowd at a comfortable distance. The refugees parted, allowing Genti and me to greet the former president. One bodyguard towered head and shoulders above everyone. Reflective aviator sunglasses shielded the direction of his gaze as he scanned the crowd. The other two well-muscled bodyguards kept a watchful eye on Mr. Berisha.

As I approached, Mr. Berisha broke into a warm smile. He extended his hand in greeting. His six-foot frame, broad shoulders, and high cheekbones signified power and prominence. Blown dried brown hair with flecks of gray covered the tops of his ears as wisps of hair fell over his forehead. Lines crinkled around his hazel eyes. He dressed in a dark suit, white shirt and dark blue tie. His firm hand grasped mine, and he bent forward to kiss me on both cheeks.

Taking his hand in greeting, I said, *"Mirëmëngjes* [good morning]. Welcome. We are honored to have you here. As you can see, everyone is excited."

"Faleminderit. Tell me about Qatrom as we tour. I want to meet with the refugee leadership as well."

Genti snapped a photo of our greeting and the surrounding crowd. He translated the questions and answers as we walked around. The bodyguards dispersed the crowd as we moved. After introducing Mr. Berisha to Sabri and other teachers, I guided Mr. Berisha to the tent where the board members waited. I left them together to discuss whatever they wished.

After an hour or so, the board escorted Mr. Berisha to his vehicle. Seeing him off, he said to me, *"Faleminderit.* I am impressed with the organization and commitment of everyone here to the welfare of all the refugees."

"Your visit meant so much to the refugees. I appreciate your time and effort to come. Your presence boosted the morale of everyone. Safe travels back to Tirana."

In a blink of an eye, Mr. Berisha and his bodyguards were gone. Yet, excitement, joy, and hope lingered over Qatrom long after their departure—a marvelous reminder that slight gestures create huge impacts.

The office telephone rang two weeks later. As Marci listened, her eyes widened; she smiled and shook her head in agreement. Something exciting was about to happen.

"Wow, Kitty Dukakis is coming. First, she will stop by the office and then tour Qatrom. She should arrive shortly after lunchtime. Joanne and I will wait here and then join you, Bobbie, for the camp tour."

"Perfect," I said. "I'll make sure our tent is uncluttered and Qatrom sparkles. I'll let the board know she is coming and tell them about her." Kitty Dukakis, the former First Lady of Massachusetts, served on the board of the Refugee Policy Center. Her primary focus was refugee and immigration legal resettlement in the United States.

After ensuring everything was in order and feeling exhausted, I stretched out on the cot in the RI tent for a quick nap. The clamor of excited voices, the scrape of the entrance gate opening, and the rumble of an engine woke me from a deep sleep. Feeling a bit disoriented, I grabbed my shoes, rubbed the sleep from my eyes, and left the tent to greet the former governor's wife. She was dressed in a suit and heels. Dark permed curls framed her almond-shaped face. She extended her hand to me and said, "I would like to discuss the organization of Qatrom before we take the tour."

"Please come inside. Would you like something to drink while we talk? We have a small food truck across from the compound that serves coffee, tea, or cold sodas."

"A cup of black coffee would be lovely. Thank you."

While she drank her coffee, we discussed the camp layout plus the role and duties of the other NGOs working in Qatrom. Women's and children's issues, their schooling and activities dominated her questions.

"I understand Albania does not have a resettlement program. Although we can house 5,000 refugees, we are only half full, as many refugees prefer to remain in Macedonia because they have a resettlement program," I said.

"I appreciate this information. Will you show me the camp, now?"

"I would be delighted. Did you stop by the office first? I was expecting Marci and Joanne to join us."

"No, we came straight here."

Our tour ended abruptly, as Kitty had an attack of food poisoning and rushed to the office to use the facilities.

Returning to the house for dinner, Marci said, "Kitty flew in here. She stayed for over two hours until her stomach settled down. We gave her rehydrating salts and Pepto-Bismol, and we called her office to tell them of her delay. I hope she will be okay. She really looked green around the edges. Stomach poisoning is not fun. How did the tour go?"

"She was impressed with everything, but the tour ended abruptly, as you know. I'm sorry about the mix up. I thought she was supposed to stop here and bring you and Joanne with her", I explained as I detected a slight edge to Marci's voice. "I'm glad you saw her. I think she was gathering information on policy to report back and help with resettlement. She is an activist and was very interested in the welfare of women and children. I think she had a favorable impression of Qatrom. Too bad the visit wasn't longer."

After a delicious dinner of goat, vegetables, and salad, we lingered over tea and discussed the visits of the two dignitaries. Humbled and honored, wrapped in our thoughts, we turned in for the night.

Rain, Rain, Rain

About 8 PM, rain and wind swirled around Korçë. The pelting rain sounded like hail against the windows, and like whips, the wind whistled and slashed the tree branches against the house. The electricity went out, and the house went dark. *I wonder what is happening in Qatrom?* We grabbed our rain gear and flashlights, jumped into the RI vehicle and sped towards Qatrom—what a mess. Rain bounced off the parched earth, the tent ropes flung their loosened stakes like whirling flags, while tent flaps smacked against themselves with booming sounds. Streams of water snaked around and threatened to enter the tents. What to do? Blankets, we had blankets. We could use them as sandbags. A conga line of humans and blankets flew from the distribution center to each tent in every section. Soggy blankets lined the tent openings and stopped the rain from leaking in. The smell of wet wool drifted through the atmosphere. The pounding of steel against steel rang out between claps of thunder as the refugees hammered the tent stakes back into the ground with whatever they could find. Everyone scurried like a colony of ants, frantically rebuilding their home after a disaster.

The 4-wheel drive vehicle got stuck in the mud between Section

2B and 3B. Indrit found a wooden plank and placed it under the stuck wheel. I ground the gears back and forth until the vehicle freed. Mud flew everywhere—the once white tents now sported a coat of wet, brown dirt. Having done all that we could to secure Qatrom, we drove to the warehouse to assess any damage. As luck would have it, water poured through holes in the roof—luckily, the leaks were not over the supplies. For the next few hours, we shoveled water from the flooded floor and draped plastic tarps over the supplies. Roof repair had to wait until the following day.

We quit at 2 AM. We were wet and exhausted, ready for a shower (hot if we were lucky), and bed—yet drenched with satisfaction and gratitude that we did all we could to secure the refugees and the supplies.

Let Me Entertain You

Boredom reigned supreme in the refugee camp. Anxieties accelerated with rumors of an impending peace settlement circulating like wildfire. Busloads of refugees arrived daily. The refugees' desire to return to Kosovo increased exponentially. But brief interludes when unexpected entertainers brought their gifts to Qatrom broke the tedium and tension.

First, Marcel, who drove me to Qatrom on my first day, was friends with a famous Albanian singer and arranged a free concert on 11 June. Sabri and friends from Dorkas erected a platform and sound equipment. Rows of school chairs provided seating for the audience. With great fanfare, the singer jumped on the stage with his two-piece band and belted out ballads and popular songs to an enthusiastic crowd of 3,000 refugees plus staff and guests. The crowd sang, clapped to the beat, tapped their feet, and danced in the aisles. Qatrom rocked for over an hour. Cheers erupted at the end of each song. Immersed in the moment, delight, tension, pain, and suffering subsided — all grateful for the brief moments of relief.

Two days later, inspired by the famous guest singer, a children's concert spontaneously started that evening. They performed the poems and songs with the emphasis on freedom and their return to Kosovo from the previous children's concert. Adults played traditional musical instruments while the crowd sang along. The songs of their homeland created a heavy, maudlin feeling like an ominous rain cloud, pregnant with water. Grabbing Elton, I went to the musicians and said, "Please play some upbeat songs for dancing."

Swiftly, the mood changed and the dancing began. Several refugees dragged me into the circle and taught me the steps and rhythm of their traditional circle dances. We laughed together as I fumbled and tripped over my feet. They encouraged me and delighted at my willingness to look awkward and go along. As dusk approached, the leaders brought me into the middle of the circle and, in English, said, "We thank you, Relief International and NATO, for all you have done for us. We ask God to watch over you always."

Their sentiment moved me to tears. I bowed in thanks, looking at each person in the eye. Words stuck in my throat as emotions gripped me. I trusted they understood my gratitude.

Next, on the evening of the 22nd, a lanky American with a contagious grin walked into Qatrom. Thirty-year-old Ed B had quit his job with a web-site-design firm and raised funds to bring karaoke to the Kosovar refugees in Albania. Qatrom was his first stop. Ed arrived with his Panasonic G700 karaoke machine, speakers, and a television monitor. I told Ed that the refugees would be delighted as many knew American songs and movies. Qatrom would rock again.

The morning brought rays of the sunbeams. A light breeze blew while Richard set up his equipment. Sabri assembled forty children to help. Adults swarmed around the karaoke tent to observe the progress. *Where did they get the electricity for the equipment?* I suspected some of the refugee electricians siphoned the electricity from the local utility poles, but other concerns of the day meant I never found the answer.

As the last touches were made, an enthusiastic but timid crowd gathered. The refugees seemed eager to attend, but not to participate. Richard, dressed in a white shirt and red athletic pants, kicked off the karaoke. He draped a long, thin arm over a willing refugee, and they sang together. But the crowd was still reluctant. So, I took the microphone, dedicating the song to their return to Kosovo by singing "Sentimental Journey" — music by Les Brown and Ben Homer, lyrics by Bud Green written in 1944 for returning WWII veterans. I sang, "Gonna take a sentimental journey... sentimental journey home..." as I strode through the audience. What I lacked in vocal quality, I made up in enthusiasm. The crowd warmed, clapped their hands, and stomped their feet. Cheers erupted when I finished. *I imagined they were all winding their way home as the words touched their hearts and dreams of returning to Kosovo.* Vjollca and her sister, both teachers, asked me to sing "Pretty Woman" with them. After that, a line formed for others to sing.

The local NGOs joined the fun. Many of them hoisted small children on their shoulders so they could watch. Again, happiness fell over the crowd. The staff took photos. A local shop in Korçë developed the film to give the refugees prints to keep as a remembrance. After the concert, Richard packed his equipment and told me that a story about karaoke in Qatrom would appear in the *New Yorker Magazine*. I learned later an article appeared in the June 21 and 28, 1999 issue.

Last but not least, in the waning days of camp, as plans for return began, Clowns without Borders arrived to entertain the children. Unfortunately, demands on my time prevented me from attending. I heard the laughter of delight as the clowns performed their magic tricks, antics, and balloon sculptures — another successful and unplanned event.

All the spontaneous, free entertainment, which broke the boredom, delighted the refugees, staff, and NGOs. Their presence interjected hope and laughter, suspended fear and provided moments of joy. I witnessed the transformation from arduous living conditions and trauma to fun and play, if only for briefly. We all needed these escapes to pause and reflect on other's unselfish goodness and kindness.

It's Over—Agreement Signed

My radio crackled—nothing but static from the poor connection. "Repeat," I said.

"Serbia signed an agreement!" came the reply.

Tears sprang to my eyes, and smiling, I announced, "The war is over!"

Elton grabbed the bullhorn, shouting, "Serbia signed an agreement!" as he ran through Qatrom. Everyone stopped what they were doing, grabbed one another, hugged, kissed, and danced for joy. Women whom I had never seen ran from their tents to embrace me. I stood outside the compound to drink in the jubilation—so emotionally exhilarating. Xhevat, my nemesis, led ten committee members to invite me to join them for coffee, their way to celebrate. Xhevat embraced me, put his arm through mine and led me to the cantina in the field next to Qatrom. Tables with umbrellas filled the area around the cantina. The refugees flooded to the site, jumping, dancing and crying with joy. Music blared from the cantina radio. Even the cantina owner joined in the dancing, swinging a towel over his head to the beat of the song. The joy rang to the heavens and shone as brightly as the sun.

Immediately, I sent word to Mehani that Serbia had signed the military agreement. Shortly, Mehani and his family arrived and walked directly towards me. He said, "I only trust you. Is the war over?"

"Yes, and I sent word to you to join us. Serbia signed the military agreement. You are free to go home." Tears of relief and joy fell from our eyes. We embraced, danced and shouted for you. Everyone in Qatrom welcomed Mehani and his family back.

Many people embraced me—all thanking me, NATO, and the United States for all we had done. In their eyes, I represented the U.S. that had saved their beloved homeland—the misplace adulation made me feel uncomfortable. Now they could return. It was all overwhelming. Everyone wanted to have a photo with me.

Xhevat approached me with his interpreter and said, "Now you must come with us to Kosovo to help us rebuild." I was stunned. My voice cracked and I nodded, "*Falemindarit.*" My heart melted. We lingered well after dusk, basking in the delight of the moment.

As I left them to enjoy their celebration, I wondered how long it would be before they could return. The nightmare of repatriation for UNHCR was about to begin. There were many questions to consider. How would UNHCR coordinate the number of refugees? What would be their plan? How long would it take? I knew the refugees would want to leave the next day. How patient would they be? Now, the waiting game would begin along with the anxiety and frustration.

Busloads of Refugees

Five busloads with two hundred people on board pulled into Qatrom at 11:00 AM. Most of the refugees were young men in good condition. Two days earlier ninety-five young, healthy men had arrived. The following day, all but seven of them had left Qatrom. Why were so many young men passing through Qatrom? Would the same happen with these new arrivals? I learned they were headed to Tirana on the pretext of joining family members. In reality, many of these men were deserters and wanted to rejoin the KLA to avoid punishment.

The cultural attitude of blood revenge lurked in the background — not only by an individual, but also by the entire family. Blood feuds were part of an ancient code of justice which dates back to the 15th century in the book of laws called the Kanun that obligates murder to be repaid by murder. Revenge was a founding principal during the reign of the Ottoman empire. After an incident the other night, the refugees agreed not to retaliate while in camp, but the promised revenge would occur when they returned to Kosovo. Such a difficult concept for me to understand. How could I identify?

I recalled times when I felt intense resentments and the desire to strike back. I battled those same tendencies within myself. Most of the time, I would withdraw or bury the feelings. "Turn the other cheek" (Matt. 5:38-42), and the concept of forgiveness, not "an eye for an eye" (Lev 24:19-21), were part of my upbringing. In my head, I heard my mother say, "If you can't say something nice, say nothing at all." I tried to put myself in the refugees' shoes. In their circumstances, could I control myself? How would I feel if I watched my family members raped or murdered? Deep in thought, I began to feel their struggle and come to terms with their cultural dictums. My heart ached. I prayed they would come to desire peace, reject their thought of revenge and rebuild Kosovo in unity.

Time would tell, but for now I suspected the KLA would renew fighting and retaliate. Many Serbian residents who lived in Kosovo chose to remain. Only the Yugoslav Military and Serbian police left Kosovo per the military agreement, known as the Kumanovo Agreement.

An Interruption

The day started when Oxfam arrived to conduct a workshop on hygiene. After the workshop, each attendee received buckets and sanitation materials. Following the workshop, the staff and volunteers set up a shoe distribution, which turned into a disaster. The refugees stormed the tent, grabbed shoes off the tables, and then threw them back because they were not Nikes. Pair after pair of shoes were separated from its mate. The shoes flew as the refugees pushed and shouted. I grabbed the bullhorn and ordered everyone out of the tent. It took two hours to pair the shoes. Next, we categorized the shoes by size and age. Later, Dorkas would help with the distribution of donated shoes for ages three to nine. I had nightmares of feeling smothered by swarming refugees. The distribution of clothes and shoes brought disorder and chaos, while other distributions were orderly. It reminded me of a feeding frenzy of piranha fish. It was scary.

Lake Ohrid

The siren call of Lake Ohrid still beckoned — a desire since I first rode into Qatrom. When an invitation from the four boys from Korçë, who worked for RI, invited Elton and me to go to the lake, I jumped at the chance. (This was shortly after the episode with Fatom and Mehani and I desperately needed a break from the tensions). We piled into Argon's family car and headed seventeen miles north to Pogradec, a town nestled between two mountain chains along Lake Ohrid's banks. Lake Ohrid didn't disappoint. The magnificent shades of cobalt blue water sparkled with sunlight. It summoned me. We arrived around noon and had lunch at a small café on the shore. After lunch, we rented a rowboat. We took turns rowing while the boys chatted. Elton joined the banter and occasionally translated for me since the boys from Korçë didn't speak English. None of that mattered. I soaked in the sun's warmth while we glided along the shoreline. I delighted in listening to them, and it was apparent that they enjoyed themselves as much as I.

After returning the boat, we headed for the sandy beach to swim. The water was cool at first, but after a few strokes, it was very refreshing. I swam out about 100 yards from shore, laid on my back, and floated, soaking in the ambiance as my body and mind relaxed. Elton swam towards me and said, "I think we should head back to shore."

Back onshore, the boys played a card game back onshore and sipped cold drinks while I sat in a chair and dried off. At 3:00 PM, we headed back to Qatrom.

We arrived in time to register two busloads for refugees from Macedonia—right back to the routine. The glow of time spent in the sun and in and on the water renewed and sustained me.

In Limbo

"*The future is something which everyone reaches at the rate of sixty minutes an hour, whatever he does, whoever he is.*"
- C. S. Lewis

Once the military agreement was signed, the refugees became impatient to return to their beloved homeland of Kosovo. They didn't want to wait for the landmines to be cleared, nor did they want to wait for the airfield to be rebuilt. They didn't want to wait for UNHCR to devise plans for repatriation, a logistical nightmare—they wanted to go home immediately.

UHNCR announced they could return to Kosovo with all the equipment, including the tents for shelter while rebuilding their homes. On 12 June, KFOR entered Kosovo with 20,000 troops, split into six brigades led by France, Germany, Italy, the United States, and two from the United Kingdom. The challenges that they faced were overwhelming and multi-faceted. The Yugoslav military and Serbian forces remained in large numbers. The KLA remained armed and visible. The fighting continued. There was no electricity or water. Bridges were down; homes were destroyed and roads were mined. Schools and hospitals were out of action.

Radio and TV stations were suspended. In addition, KFOR had to ensure a military vacuum did not ensue as the Yugoslav military and Serb forces evacuated before a civil authority. United Nations Interim Administration in Kosovo (UNMIK) had time to form. The UN Security Council mandated UNMIK to establish four pillars: 1. Humanitarian services, aid and oversight conducted by UNHCR 2. A UN civil administration 3. Institutional building by OSCE and 4. Reconstruction by the European Union.

Meanwhile, UNHCR began sending convoys carrying blankets, mattresses, tents, plastic sheeting and hygiene kits to Peja (Pec), Prizren and Pristina. It organized the local authorities and KFOR to rebuild the air strip at Korçë to air vac the refugees in southern Albania. In Qatrom, refugees searched for trucks, drivers or anyone willing to drive to Kosovo. Unfortunately, many remained in camp since their money was stolen by scam artists — not right!

Kosovar, one of our teenage volunteers, came to me and asked permission to work at the airstrip. He said it was an opportunity for him and the other teenage boys to earn money. I thanked him for asking me and said they should take the job offer. I would welcome them back when the airstrip was finished.

Days were more hectic without all of the volunteers, but we managed. One afternoon after a distribution, I found Drita and Yeta sobbing. I saw Xhilda and asked her to join me in talking with them. Between sobs and tears, they said they dreaded the separation when they went home. They lived in separate villages without public transportation. How could they remain friends and communicate without telephones or the internet? Xhilda and I listened to their grief, listened to the deep sobs that come from the hollow emptiness of loss. Their friendship developed into a strong bond at Qatrom — they were inseparable. Living with another unexpected loss was almost more than they could bear. Xhilda and I enveloped them in our arms and wept with them. Again, my heart wrenched. Again, I had no answers.

What to Expect—A Conversation with My Son, Will, 24 June 1999

Concerns dominated my mind after the military agreement was signed. Why did busload after busload of men arrive at Qatrom from Macedonia? Why did they stay for just one night before traveling to Tirana or Durrës? What dangers lurked in Kosovo for the returnees? Would skirmish flare up? Who would disarm the armies? I needed to talk with Will for some answers.

"Hi Will. Could you answer the questions I have swirling in my head? The military agreement did not include Kosovo as an independent state. Will fighting resume as the KLA increase in number?"

"If Kosovo holds to form, the killings will start now. According to Charles Tilly, a sociologist, 'Violence was highest during the consolidation of a state, not its collapse.'"

"That doesn't sound encouraging. What about disarmament?"

"With NATO there, I think the Kosovo's state-building death toll will be lower than the war death toll. There will be revenge killings, but I think most will be one, state-building and two, opportunism."

"What are the risks involved? I can't help but think what will happen to the refugees when they leave here."

"First, without a formal government, there needs to be state building. The KLA is likely to break into factions as various people compete to be the head of the military, the presidency, etc. Second, the KLA is likely to turn to guerrilla style warfare as they struggle against NATO. Especially if they believe the NATO countries have little patience for bloodshed. As of now, two British soldiers are dead. The key to success is disarmament, which will not be easy. A third possibility is that organized crime will take over during the chaos and void, as noted in many of the newly formed states after the Soviet Union breakup."

"What do you mean by opportunism?"

"Opportunism can be carried out by individuals, families, and small groups who realize that the penalties for being caught for stealing Serb possessions or killing a Serb are low. NATO has many challenges to impose order, disarm the KLA, remove the Yugoslav and Serbian forces, and keep peace. In addition, it is necessary to remove the landmines. NATO is under so much pressure and in the spotlight with the global media watching and reporting. My best guess is the next three weeks or so are critical. If NATO sends the message that everyone is likely to be caught and punished, which was not the case in week one, then opportunism can be squashed. If NATO can disarm the KLA bands, then the state-building competition can be done without bloodshed. Neither task is easy."

"Wow, Will, there is so much to contemplate. I did not know the complexities. It seems overwhelming to me. Let's hope that NATO is up for the task."

This discussion remained in my thoughts, as many of the refugees prepared to return to Kosovo. Before their return, the NATO forces moved into Kosovo to remove landmines along the returning routes. How successful they would be, as so many landmines still kill and maim innocent people in Cambodia and Vietnam? Anguished thoughts lingered in my head. I longed to help them rebuild their beloved homeland. For now, I had to concentrate on the task at hand, as it would be weeks before the refugees could return.

Landmine Training

We want to go home! What is taking so long? When the military agreement was signed, it called for the withdrawal of Serbian forces from Kosovo and mandated removing all landmines, which did not happen. The last vestige of defeat and a continuation of the harm done during the conflict.

Fear for the refugees' safe return somewhat subsided in me when UNHCR developed plans to train all Kosovar refugees on landmines before they returned to their homeland. At Qatrom on 17 June, each family received a landmine brochure, which described various types of landmines and the danger. On 24 June, Save the Children, an NGO working in Korçë, sent a representative to Qatrom to train the teachers on landmines. The teachers educated the children on the size, shape, and dangers of landmines. That Saturday, a major from the French NATO planted dummy landmines in the vacant field near the camp. All 3,000 refugees had to take the training on landmines and how to identify them.

The air was still on the hot days at the end of June. Day after day, the relentless sun beat down on the long queues of refugees. They entered the dummy landmine field. Here they could learn in a safe, controlled environment, but on the journey home, a wrong step on an undetected ordinance could be disastrous. They could be maimed or killed. As part of the training, they were given photos and descriptions of landmines, cluster bomblets, and other types of munitions. Their hearts pounded and they kept their eyes glued to the ground as each person stepped cautiously through the field. The French KFOR kept a watchful eye on the proceedings, alert and ready to assist.

I watched as they scattered and picked their way through the grass, trying to detect the hidden and buried ordnances without tripping a wire or stepping on one. The air tingled with tension. The parents' stern voices echoed over the field, trying to keep their children in check and not run—serious business. A shriek sounded as someone tripped over a hidden wire or took a wrong step and heard a click. Everyone froze. The first rule: don't move. Stand still until someone comes. The major arrived on the scene to assist as others gathered around him. They looked somber and fearful as they realized the magnitude of the danger. By the end of the day, everyone was hot, tired, and sweaty. There were heavy sighs as they finished the training with evening approaching. It took many days for 3,000 refugees to file through the minefield before returning to their tents to pack and to contemplate the dangers that lay ahead.

Despite the efforts of British KFOR and other KFOR forces to disarm the landmines, anger and fear welled up in me almost to the point of explosion as I contemplated the return trip home for these refugees. Unsafe roadside routes filled with documented and undocumented landmines lay ahead. Serbian troops planted more before they withdrew from Kosovo to continue the pain and suffering in absentia. The number of unexploded bomblets, anti-tank, and anti-personnel mines remained long after the conflict ended. Besides, many unexploded cluster bombs remained in Kosovo from the NATO bombing. Danger lurked everywhere. The mines often shifted with the change of season, meaning documentation could be inaccurate. Having taken part in landmine training, I understood the dangers and pitfalls of weapons of war meant to explode, kill, maim, and destroy, often buried from view, to create havoc and chaos, grief, and pain. Per international law, all minefields consisting of twenty or more landmines required documentation on maps—less than twenty not mandatory.

(Seventy-eight countries are contaminated with landmines, while approximately 15,000 people, mainly children and civilians, are killed each year. In 1977, the Ottawa Treaty banned stockpiling, production, and transfer of anti-personnel mines. One hundred sixty-four nations signed the treaty. The United States, Russia, and China did not—*why*? The sale of landmines is very profitable.)

The Last Night

"Challenges are what make life interesting, overcoming them is what makes life meaningful."

- Joshua J. Merine

Too impatient to wait for UNCHR to organize the return to Kosovo, most of the refugees with some money and influence arranged private transport. By 6 July, everyone was gone except for about a dozen families who remained scattered throughout the Qatrom — none of the remaining families could afford personal transport. Security for the remaining refugees demanded a solution. Scattered throughout the camp increased the threat of violence or theft by the local population. We decided to assemble everyone into the large community tent in the RI compound for their safety. The security guards could keep a watchful eye on the tent. I sent Genti, Elton, Indrit, and Xhilda to inform the families to collect their belonging and bring them to the community tent for this last night. I instructed them to explain it was for their safety and the safety of their belongings. One by one, the families moved their belongings to the tent — back and forth until everything and everyone gathered. The Salvation

Army prepared the evening meal as always, and the refugees ate together as one big family.

At dusk, we gathered outside the tent to chat. Per usual, the men, dressed in tracksuit pants and buttoned shirts or light jackets over t-shirts, sat at the tables and benches. The women sat on the ground. The women wore long, ankle-length full skirts, short sleeved cotton t-shirts under long-sleeved, buttoned shirts, often with shawls draped over their shoulders and head coverings. The coverings, signifying tribal affiliation, were tight-fitting caps made of wool and molded to fit the crown.

Never wanting to miss an opportunity to do a bit of cross-cultural training, I told the men that in the United States, men give up their seats for the women. Horror shadowed their faces; they shook their heads, as if saying, "No way." With a twinkle in my eye and a smile on my face, I nodded toward the women and said, "It would be thoughtful for you to offer your seats to the women."

The men looked at me with narrowed eyes, gazed towards the women, hesitated, then stood, offering up their seats to the women. The women looked shocked. Then giggles rippled through the group of women as they rose from the ground and walked to the tables. They whispered *"Faleminderit"*, as they brushed past me. They seemed delighted and surprised. Elton and Xhilda gave me a wink and a high-five. I gave a respectful bow to the men and told them, *"Faleminderit."* The moment was interrupted by the buzz of children running around. Soon it would be their bedtime and time for us to leave. The security team had just arrived. I told them to be extra watchful since all the refugees were gathered in the community tent for safety.

As the dark of night approached, I turned to the refugees and said, *"Naten e mire"* [goodnight].

When I turned to leave, one older woman, face worn with fatigue and worry, pulled her shawl around her. She touched my arm and in a trembling voice, she said, "I am afraid to go home."

"Why?" I asked.

Silent tears streamed down her face. Clutching at her dress, she cried, "I was separated from my family in the mountains as we were escaping. I am afraid to go home. I am afraid I will find them all *dead*."

I had no words. Murmuring, "*Më vjen keq*," [I'm sorry], I wrapped my arms around the frightened woman. She buried her head in my shoulder, and her body trembled and her tears flowed. We both wept and clung together for support and comfort—neither one of us wanting to let go but to gather strength from each other. I said a silent prayer that she would find her family safe and the fear that gripped her would ease. I could not imagine her pain and to this day wondered what happened to her—did she ever reunite with her family? Hope was all I had.

Sleep eluded me that night—my thoughts raged: *how will they integrate the imprints of suffering into their lives? How will they rebuild their beloved Kosovo now a charred land?*

Dawn approached. The remaining refugees were about to embark on their journey home. My head filled with words of encouragement, admiration, and blessing. Each refugee left a mark on my heart, which swelled with love, compassion, and acceptance. As gratitude filled me to my core, I silently thanked RI for the opportunity to live and grow with these beautiful and loving people. After breakfast, I returned to Qatrom for one last goodbye.

I meditated on the following quotation by Mother Teresa, "It's not how much you do, but how much love you put in what you do that counts."

Waving Goodbye

"Only in the agony of parting do we look into the depths of love."
- George Elliot

Departure day, 7 July — I walked along the familiar road, saying goodbye and wishing the remaining refugees well as they waited anxiously for the French KFOR truck to take them to the airstrip. With a furrowed brow and puzzled look, a male refugee stopped me and asked, "Why would you leave America to be with us?"

Surprised, I placed my hands over my heart and replied, "I feel honored and humbled to have been able to serve you and God. All of you have enriched my life in so many ways. *Faleminderit.*"

Tears spilled from his eyes and trickled down his cheek. A slight smile curled around his lips. He bowed and said, "*Po, Faleminderit.*" His cheeks flushed as he turned and hastened back to his family.

Alone, I watched the last French NATO truck drive away. Tears blurred my vision. Trails of dust clouded their smiles and waves of goodbye — the trucks fading in the distance. My heart throbbed. Emotions struck me like a thunderbolt — thrilled for them as they embarked on their way to a devastated Kosovo. Fear filled me when I thought of landmines and bombs which could explode along the road. Hope for them quelled the fear as I thought of them rebuilding their nation, free from Serbia's aggression. I felt gratitude for my challenging and enriching experience.

A visceral, eerie feeling of emptiness settled over Qatrom. Everything was gone except the trash, pit latrines, shower tents, and water taps. A hollowness seeped into me as my emotions drained and fatigue set in. Yet, the words of Robert Emmons in his book, *Thanks*, drifted into my thoughts "Gratitude is the way the heart remembers—remembers the kindnesses, the cherished interactions with others, compassionate actions of strangers, surprising gifts, and everyday blessings. By remembering, we honor and acknowledge the many ways in which who and what we are has been shaped by others, both living and dead."

Those three months felt like a whirlwind, filled with knowns and unknowns, chaos and calm, success and failure, yet they provided me with an oasis of loving and nurturing to give and receive. Amid the swirl of activities, time still stood for grief, kindness, and joy. With a humbled, enriched, and grateful heart, I acknowledged the humanness of us. Differences dissolved longing for the same things—love, security, and peace bonded us indefinitely.

Although the daunting task of camp cleanup loomed large on the horizon, I took time to reflect on all that happened. In my reverie, my mind flashed forward with thoughts of working in Kosovo. Time would tell if I could join the returned refugees in their beloved homeland.

A Promise Kept

Cleanup was completed and warehouses emptied. Unused supplies were donated or shipped to Kosovo. I was thoroughly exhausted, but I had time on my hands before my return flight to the United States and my reunion with family and friends.

Remembering I wanted to go to Durrës, a port city on the Adriatic Sea, Genti called his relatives there. They invited us to visit. On Tuesday, 20 July, Genti arranged the excursion from Korçë to Durrës. After a long, hot four-hour bus ride over bumpy roads, we arrived. Genti's aunt and uncle greeted me with warmth and grace. Their second-floor apartment and balcony faced the sea. A gentle breeze blew through the living space. The apartment sparkled clean and bright with loving care and personal touches. An atmosphere of kindness and welcome pervaded. Genti's relatives insisted I sleep in their bedroom while they slept on the sofa. With a pleading look, I turned to Genti for direction. He said in English, "You will insult them if you refuse."

Smiling, I turned to his aunt and uncle, saying, "*Faleminderit.*"

We were on the coast, so all we wanted was a fresh fish meal. Genti found a delightful restaurant where all the local people assembled to chat and eat. The hum of voices stopped as we entered—all eyes riveted on me.

"Genti, why is everyone staring at me?" I asked.

Genti laughed, "They are not used to seeing a foreigner."

Slightly uncomfortable, I nodded and flashed a quick smile at everyone before scurrying to a table in the corner. Lighted candles in beer bottles decorated red and white checked tablecloths. Fishing nets, buoys, and fishing traps hung on the walls, creating a friendly atmosphere of a fishing port. The limited menu contained Albanian cuisine and the catch of the day. We ordered fresh fish and a bottle of white wine, and eventually the local people stopped staring and resumed their chatter and laughter.

The meal was delicious. Satisfied and relaxed, Genti and I returned to the apartment for a conversation with his aunt and uncle. Genti, as an interpreter, spoke about their lives in the port city and their new freedoms after the fall of Communism.

"What is different now for you?" I asked.

"We love having access to material things, like washing machines, but it is difficult to pay for rent. We always had free rent under communism," his uncle said. "We can ship our fish throughout the country now. With the demand, our wages are better. We would like to have more tourists which would help the local business. We are working on it."

Feeling fatigued, I said, "*Faleminderit, Natën e mirë.* [Thank you and good night]. I think Durrës is a lovely port town. I hope more people can visit." As I prepared for bed, I reflected on the blissful and tranquil lives of Genti's relatives compared to the chaos of the refugee camp. I marveled at the simple, unhurried life in this town, which was completely untouched by the flurry of refugees flooding the border on the other side of Albania. Even with its beautiful coastline with white sand and azure colored water, Durrës remained devoid of tourism. The local population enjoyed the lively fishing port and the remnants of Greek and Roman architecture. Albania was not on the tourist map. After spending an evening in the home of this congenial and generous family, I fell into a deep, restful sleep. Their home was a perfect place for me to unwind.

Following breakfast, Genti and I carried beach chairs, blankets, and a beach umbrella to the soft white sand along the Adriatic Sea. The smell of salt air, the cry of gulls overhead, the warm sun on our shoulders, a gentle breeze kissing our cheeks, and the steady sound of the waves lapping on the shore lulled me into a state of euphoria. After setting up, Genti and I walked along the shoreline. A sense of unease washed over me when I noticed that once again, I was the focus of attention for other beachgoers. *What is going on?* "Genti, why is everyone staring so intently at me? I am feeling more uncomfortable than I did last night."

"Very few foreigners come here. You stand out like a sore thumb to them — they are curious and suspicious."

Still puzzled, I asked, "How do they know I am a foreigner?"

Laughing, Genti said, "We can tell the difference between the various ethnic groups here. It is easy for us to spot a non-Albanian."

"Wow," I said, "America is such a melting pot of nationalities. When I sit around the table at UNHCR or elsewhere, it could be a cross-section of the U.S. I love the diversity. I am uncomfortable with the stares. In the states, it is impolite to stare — again, a cultural difference. Let's head back to the blankets."

After a swim, I fell sound asleep under the umbrella. Genti woke me nearly two hours later and said, "We need to get back to the apartment, then catch the bus back to Korçë."

After a reluctant goodbye, we headed to the bus station. The eerie feeling of being watched lingered with me on the bus ride back and beyond. I had gained a greater understanding of the origin of the stares, albeit the constant watchful eyes never ceased to be unnerving.

I had a few days left in Korçë before heading to Tirana to give my final report to RI. Genti also lingered, even though he was free to return to Tirana. I suspected that he and Xhilda had become an item — how perfect. Two gentle, kind souls, one from Tirana, one from Korçë, met in Qatrom. I wonder if their budding relationship lasted. Maybe one day I would find out.

Again, I marveled at the thoughtfulness of the young Albanians. They radiated warmth and kindness. I will carry memories of them forever in my heart, hoping one day we will reconnect.

Homeward Bound

> *"They said their goodbye, and in their farewell, there was also a welcome."*
>
> *- Mario Benedetti*

Why were goodbyes so hard? Goodbyes meant transitions. All transitions required energy — energy sucked from me and leaving me empty. A duality of emotions gripped me with an iron fist — not wanting to leave the intense bonds I had made and dreading the empty feelings of goodbye versus the longing to be with my sons and grandchildren, family members and friends. Having done this before, I knew what was ahead. The reverse culture shock of re-entering my home in the U.S. with its overabundance of material trappings and superficial conversations contrasted sharply with the minimal supplies in Qatrom Refugee Camp and the town of Korçë and the deep emotional bonds I made with the refugees and staff. Witnessing the pain and suffering of the refugees, listening to their stories, and the chaos and intensity of humanitarian work juxtaposed against the phatic discourse at home. I needed to talk, decompress, discuss my emotions and intense passion for the work and the plight of the people forced from their homeland. No one wanted to listen. I wanted to scream. How is it possible to dismiss or be unaware of the suffering of other human beings? Why do we ignore it in the United States? Why are we wrapped up in our myopic world where we cannot or won't see the plight of others? Will, at least, listened and asked provoking questions, pouring a salve over my aching heart. No one else wanted to listen. I dreaded the emptiness that would prevail. How would I fill the void once my fatigue subsided? What would I do after visiting my family and friends after attending the family reunion in Maine?

First, I searched for other humanitarian opportunities. I had four interviews with World Vision to work in Albania. The process ended abruptly when the country manager married and left on his honeymoon—another void. I was familiar with this emptiness—it had set in before when my mission in Zambia ended abruptly in 1997. Shortly after my return from Zambia, I had the opportunity to celebrate my 58th birthday by working for two weeks with Mayan women in Guatemala, where the effects of a thirty-six-year war still lingered. After visiting many humanitarian groups throughout Guatemala, we spent five days at a retreat center with thirteen Mayan women. The cost of our trip funded one of the Mayan women to attend the retreat. Within the five days, we implemented several meditative techniques, such as Tai Chi and mindfulness, dyads, group activities, and other healing methods to help the women cope with the aftermath of war. At the end of the retreat, they expressed their gratitude for being allowed to discuss the war, their feelings, fears, and anxiety of not knowing whether their loved ones were dead or alive. In the Mayan culture, such discussions were taboo. This amazing experience reinforced my commitment to help others.

The desire to work with refugees burned on like an unquenchable flame in my heart after my return from Qatrom. To fill the gap, I researched coping with change and how to journal for the next several months. After researching, I developed workshops for refugees dealing with change and self-published a guided journal book for refugees entitled *Reflections*. The book had three versions—English, Albanian, and French. I conducted workshops in Chicago with Refugee One, an NGO where my former boss in Kenya was the managing director. Through them, I located several Albanian communities and donated the journaling books to them. The feedback I received encouraged me to continue working with refugees.

Researching and writing aided my re-entry process in coping with change. I also used the journal book to write and reflect. Yet, the flame of my longing to be in Kosovo flickered on. I continued to surf the internet for openings. An opportunity came in September 2000 to serve as the reporting officer with UNHCR to report on the Kosovo Women's Initiative Program (KWI). The U.S. Department of State had given $10,000,000 to mitigate the suffering of women after the war. My fingers flew over the application and within minutes, I hit the send button. I waited and waited for a response. Finally, a telephone interview came — followed by another waiting period. Would I ever hear?

At last, an offer came. The head of mission in Kosovo selected me based on my experience working with refugees over younger women with university degrees in women's studies. I felt relieved and thrilled to be going to Kosovo — my heart filled with anticipation and excitement. My mind flashed back to Qatrom, the people I had met, and the burning desire to accompany the refugees as they returned home.

By accepting the position, I would witness their recovery and rebuilding. Again, an opportunity, a new chapter, a new beginning had blessed me. What challenges lay ahead for me? Would I reconnect with some refugees from Qatrom? I certainly hoped so — what a reunion it would be. I couldn't wait to get on the plane for Pristina. Once there, I met with the director and assistant director of the Bureau of Population, Refugees and Migration (PRM), the humanitarian bureau of the State Department. The director explained the reports the State Department wanted — monthly updates of the women's programs, the successes, the failures, and where to improve. I looked forward to traveling around Kosovo to meet with the women and their groups and reconnect with these beautiful people. A month after I arrived in Kosovo, I celebrated my 61st birthday. I had answered the call of my heart and was filled with gratitude for the opportunity to serve others once again.

> *"It is within my power to either serve God or not to serve Him. Serving Him, I add to my own good and the good of the whole world. Not serving Him, I forfeit my own good and deprive the world of that good which was in my power to create."*
>
> - Leo Tolstoy

Acknowledgements

First, I want to thank Will, his colleagues and my friends for their encouragement to write about my refugee and humanitarian experiences. I have stories, but I never thought of myself as a writer. I appreciate the insistence and push, although uncomfortable at times.

Thank you to Betty Jo Buro, June O'Brian and Gina Hogan Edwards for your classes and workshops in learning the craft of writing. Without your guidance and encouragement, I would not know how to write a book. I appreciate David Ferris for his excellent editing, careful and thoughtful critiques that urged me to dig deeper. Thank you to Alexa Nazzaro of Aaxel Author Services for holding my hand and guiding me through the publishing process along with your team, Stéphane Pigeon and Deividas Jablonskis.

Deep appreciation to my friends, who read and corrected my vignettes: Nancy Williamson, your way with words, Sandra Wylie, your creative writing skills, and Aggie Bell, your English teacher's expertise. Your suggestions improved my writing in so many ways.

Most profoundly, I thank Relief International, the Kosovar refugees and my interpreters — you opened my heart. I grew in love and compassion working with you. I am forever grateful for the opportunity to grow and love more deeply as I witnessed human suffering, home and family, hope and perseverance, and the refugees' courage in the face of unbelievable trauma, horror and adversity. Heartfelt thank you to my interpreters, Elton, Xhilda, Genti and Indrit, whose tireless commitment allowed me to communicate with the refugees. I treasure the bonds and closeness we shared. You are forever in my heart.

Thank you to social media, for in 2021 I was able to reconnect with Xhilda, Genti and Elton after 21 years. My heart is full knowing they are well and successful. As an aside—Xhilda and Genti, who met and fell in love at Qatrom Refugee Camp, are happily married with two children. Eton immigrated to the U.S. and is reunited with his family, married and has a beautiful teenage daughter. I love happy endings.

Roberta Lord spent eleven years working overseas in the humanitarian field, where her focus was working with refugees in Kenya, Albania, Kosovo, and Guatemala as well as village men and women in Zambia. With Relief International under the umbrella of UNCHR, she served as camp manager at the Qatrom Refugee Camp in Albania, where the refugees nicknamed her "Mother of the Camp."

Bobbie also facilitated workshops in the United States, including at Princess Basma Centre for Disabled Children in Jerusalem, where she developed a program for the mothers of disabled children, and at Interfaith Refugee and Immigration Ministries in Chicago, where she assisted resettled refugee and immigrant women in improving their lives through social and economic development. She also has been a guest lecturer to many organizations including various women's clubs, Rotary Clubs, and church groups.

No longer working overseas, she continues to empower young women while working as a house director in sororities on university campuses.

Bobbie considers herself foremost a humanitarian supporting those who have no voice. *Without a Homeland* is her first book. She can be reached at www.bobbielord.com

Made in the USA
Columbia, SC
02 July 2023